Your Strong-Willed Child

A Positive Discipline Guide to Calm Your
Strong-Willed Child Without
Extinguishing Their Inner Fire

Jordan Waldrop

contained within this document, including, but not limited to, errors, omissions, or inaccuracies.

Table of Contents

Introduction

"Children need love, especially when they do not deserve it"

-by Harold S. Hulbert

Does your child seem to have a will cast of pure iron? Take a moment to think about your child and whether they exhibit the following:

- Do they have angry outbursts?
- Are they impatient?
- Do they continually ask "but why?" to any rules you set or limitations you place on their behavior?
- Does your child try to make up their own rules?
- Do they insist on moving and living at a pace that they dictate?
- Does your child seem to argue at any given opportunity?
- Are they impatient?
- Do they have a tendency to be bossy?
- Can your child at times be as stubborn as an ox?
- Do they regularly confuse what they need with what they want?
- Does your child have selective listening and ignore your warnings about misbehavior?

If you can identify these traits within your own child, you may have a strong-willed child on your hands.

Strong-willed children present parents across the globe with a variety of challenges when it comes to child-rearing. They make their mild-mannered peers seem like little angels, and you may find yourself envious of their parents. However, you don't have a bad child on your hands. You have a child with a strong will, and that isn't a bad thing either.

Strong-willed children are sometimes called exuberant. They often have a high-energy level that leaves you wondering how it seems like you can't even see them whizzing around. They are passionate; they seem to be able to argue any lawyer under the table, even if they're wrong. They get creative, sometimes in a good way, and sometimes in misbehavior. Strong-willed children are often misunderstood by both their parents and society. They are labeled as difficult, or even bad, kids. This is further than the truth than the Arctic and Antarctic poles are from each other. These children are hidden treasures that just need those around them to understand and adjust their interaction with them accordingly.

Perhaps this is your struggle, and you want to read this book because you have such a child on your hands. You may either be at your wit's end or simply trying to understand them better. Learning about your child and how to handle them is the first step toward making your job as a parent easier and bringing out the best in your child. If you are seeking answers, we're here to help you find them. This book covers a wide range of parenting topics, including:

- Discovering an understanding of your strong-willed child.
- Figuring out what your child's temperament is and how that affects both them and your interaction with them.
- Learning what parenting style best suits your child.
- How to get your child to cooperate with you.
- How to use positive discipline to enforce your family rules.
- How to set family rules and what kinds of rules should be set.
- How to build a trusting relationship with your child.
- What behavior is appropriate for your child's age.
- How having a strong-willed child is actually a good thing.

Yes, you read that correctly. Having a child that society labels as difficult is a good thing? The answer to that question is a resounding, "Yes!"

Once you can understand your strong-willed child, their needs, what motivates them, and how to handle them, your job as a parent doesn't seem as intimidating or daunting anymore. Strong-willed children aren't like other children, and that is actually a great thing. They have so much potential, they can achieve so much success, they can bring you so much joy, and they can make you the proudest parent on the planet. All they need is to be understood and be given the right environment, the right parenting, and the right developmental tools to flourish.

Your child isn't inherently a bad child and it's your job to understand why they are such a blessing and how to bring out the best in them. If you want answers to your burning questions as the parent of an exuberant or strong-willed child, keep reading. You'll learn everything you need to know to make your parenting job easier, and to make their personality shine so that society has to eat their words when labeling your pride and joy as a bad kid.

About the Author

Jordan Waldrop understands the struggles of every parent who has a strong-willed child. Being the parent of just such an exuberant child, he has had years of experience of dealing with a child with an iron will. A desire to understand his child and to know how to deal with them in a way that would bring out the best in them made Jordan seek out information. He has spent many countless hours, days, and months doing all the research possible on the subject of raising a strong-willed child. One subject in particular—that of discipline—can be dreaded by every parent, even when they have what seems to be an angelic child. But when Jordan discovered the art of positive discipline, a new world opened up! Suddenly discipline wasn't about anger, frustration, and negative punishment anymore. Responsiveness increased with positive reinforcement and knowing how to build a relationship based on trust and open communication. Suddenly parenting became easier, and all of that constant anger and frustration melted away.

Jordan has been where you are, asked the questions that you are asking, and experienced the self-doubt and feelings of hopelessness that many parents of strong-willed children go through. Now it's time to share that knowledge and experience with the world. In a bid to help other parents avoid the pitfalls, overcome the obstacles, and nurture a well-adjusted and well-behaved spirited child without breaking their spirit, this book has been written. Out of a passion for children and an understanding of the difficulties faced by the parents of exuberant children, all the knowledge gained has been laid out to help you be the best parent you can be and bring out your child's true and full potential.

Chapter 1:

Discipline, Who?

Children act out all the time, you can see it almost everywhere you go; shopping centers, play parks, even in the homes of friends and family. The behavior manifests itself in many different ways. Kids may shout, draw on the walls, throw themselves writhing on the floor, or even physically lash out by hitting or kicking someone. A child acting out is not an uncommon phenomenon, but sometimes parents may feel powerless to stop the behavior. For the most part, we see a child acting out as simply being unruly or naughty, and the way we respond is in accordance with that belief. However, what if the behavior is more deeply rooted than we realize?

What if we don't look at acting out as the problem but rather as a symptom? To successfully understand acting out, you need to view the behavior as a means of communication.

Reasons for Acting Out

A child who is acting out isn't necessarily doing it on purpose to push your buttons or provoke a reaction. The behavior is their natural expression of an internal state of being. Let's look at some of the reasons a child may be acting out.

Tiredness

Every parent probably knows this one. Children enjoy playing and may not want to stop, even when they are tired. They may even fight being put down for a nap!

Anger

Just as with tiredness, this is a common reason for children to act out.

Hunger

The term 'hangry' has been coined in recent years and there's a very good reason for that. People become naturally irritable when they are hungry because of their low blood sugar.

Needing to Pee

This is often not realized by parents. When a child isn't independently using the potty, they may hold their pee and become grouchy as a result of physical discomfort.

External Influences

Children absorb stimuli and information like a sponge and they often copycat external input, such as seeing other children acting out in real life or through TV programs. They may even be copying you and the way you behave when you lose your temper. Copycatting is a natural behavior for children and they may not understand that the behavior is not acceptable, because they see others doing it.

Anxiety

Unlike adults, children are often not able to express worry, fear, or stress and this may lead to meltdowns, as they can't identify and recover from these highly negative emotions.

Sadness

We like to see children as being perpetually happy with a never-ending sunny disposition, but this isn't always the case. Children experience sadness for a variety of reasons; sometimes they may even become sad about something we expect them to be happy about, and we overlook their sadness.

Curiosity

Children are infinitely curious about the world around them and learn through first hand sensory learning. They may be playing and learning about the things around them in a misguided way, such as pushing objects off surfaces to see what happens, without even realizing the behavior isn't appropriate.

Frustration

When a child is attempting to learn something, they may become deeply frustrated when their attempts to master a task fail, especially if they have been trying over and over again.

They Don't Realize It's Unacceptable

Children sometimes just don't understand or know that a behavior is unacceptable even though you, as an adult, see it as a 'no-brainer.'

Not Understanding Limits

Children may not understand the reason or logic behind the limits we set for them. Their disobedience to your rules for them may be due to not understanding why they should or should not do something.

Confusion

When setting limitations or rules for our children, it's very important to be extremely clear about what is expected and why, to avoid confusion. For this to happen you need to be clear and free of confusion yourself; otherwise, you may be sending a signal to your child that specific behavior is acceptable.

Inconsistency

Children function best when there is a strong sense of predictability, routine, and consistency in their lives. This offers them a sense of security. Feeling insecure may lead to acting out due to the uncertainty of their daily lives, and what or how things are going to happen.

Inconsistent reinforcement of rules and limitations may also lead to crabbiness due to confusion over where they stand on the matter.

Over-Controlling Parenting

When we run our homes under strict control over every little thing, children may feel overly pressured. They may also feel like they are not getting the support they need to meet our expectations. They may act out as a way to gain some autonomy.

Overstimulation

Children learn through sensory stimuli. If they are presented with an overwhelming amount of stimuli, such as too much noise, too many people, or even too much color around them, they may act out because they cannot cope with the overstimulation.

Testing Limits

If we aren't confident authority figures in our children's lives, acting out may be a way to test the limits of what they can and cannot do based on our uncertain or shaky exertion of authority.

Inability to Express Themselves

As you can see, many of the reasons children may act out are due to the inability to express themselves verbally or in healthy ways. They may not understand their emotions, or even realize that they are experiencing these emotions. In these instances, acting out is their natural way of expressing a variety of emotions, or even physical experiences, such as stress, fear, anxiety, or physical discomfort, to name a few. It is important that we try to look deeper than the behavior and see it as the symptom of something more. It is our job to try to find the reason why they are acting out so that we can understand how to handle them.

That being said, just because you can understand the root cause of your child's acting out doesn't mean that you can overlook the behavior. Discipline is a vital part of a child's development, and you need to step up to the plate to provide them with what they need.

Why Discipline Is Important

Discipline isn't just about providing your child with the consequences for their actions; discipline is an integral part of teaching them life skills that will benefit and help them to grow up to be responsible adults. Neglecting to discipline your child isn't doing them a kindness or being 'nice' to them, it actually equates to neglecting them.

Discipline takes on many forms, depending on your parenting style, but regardless of how you choose to discipline your child, it is necessary and it offers your child various benefits. It is also important to take stock of the difference between punishment and consequence. We often make the mistake of viewing both as the same thing, but they are far from each other! Using appropriate consequences for a specific action can teach a child to learn from a mistake, whereas punishments may teach them how to misbehave without being caught.

For discipline to be effective and not cause confusion or outright rebellion, it is important that you clearly explain the reasons for rules and limits in a way that your child understands. If they do not understand the reasoning behind the limitation, they may be more likely to ignore it.

Safety

Offering your child consequences for unsafe behavior, such as riding the bicycle in the road, teaches them to make safer choices. This not only helps them learn, but it also ensures that they are doing their best to stay safe even when you are not around.

Decision Making

Discipline affects a child's ability to make good decisions or the right choices in life. You are teaching them important skills such as problem-solving, self-regulation, and impulse control. For example, taking away TV privileges as a result of watching television instead of doing homework helps to instill a sense of responsibility. Taking away bicycle privileges for riding their bike in the road helps teach them to make safer choices down the line.

Anxiety Management

Contrary to what you may believe, when your tantrum-ing toddler is being bossy and trying to exert themselves as the figure of authority instead of you, they don't actually want to be in control. I know, that just doesn't match up, right? What may be happening is that a child is testing the limits as a way to reassure themselves that the caregiver is able to keep them safe. When you offer your child too much free rein, they may experience anxiety. This anxiety stems from having to make their own decisions, as well as insufficient leadership and guidance. When you offer a child consequences to their actions, both positive and negative, they are able to learn and develop vital interpersonal life skills.

Managing Emotions

Disciplining a child for inappropriate expressions of emotion helps them to learn how to manage those emotions. For instance, you may enforce a time-out for emotional outbursts or physically lashing out as an emotional response to a stimulus. This is a great way to teach a child to remove themselves from the situation until they have their emotions under control and can respond in an appropriate way.

Discipline to help manage emotions may also be positive reinforcement. When praising a child for continuing to try to accomplish something, despite experiencing setbacks, it helps them learn how to deal with the frustration they are feeling at not being able to get it right.

Yet another way in which to use discipline to encourage appropriate emotional responses and management is to ignore milder acting out. If your child throws a temper tantrum, ignoring the behavior may teach them that it is not an appropriate means of having their needs met.

The 'Perfect' Child Is a Myth

When it comes to childrearing, the word 'perfect' should be erased from your parenting dictionary. There is no such thing as the perfect parent! There is no such thing as the perfect child! Think of these as mythological concepts; we may like to fantasize about them, but it's never going to happen.

Adults look at children with the preconceived notion of happiness, bubbliness, smiles, and constant good moods. This, however, couldn't be further from the truth. Take a moment to consider how you think about or view adults. You see them as regular people with their good qualities and their flaws, right? Well, you should learn to view children in the same way. They have their good days and their bad days, just like adults. You will never find a child that is 100% obedient and is permanently in a happy mood.

If the 'fantasy' child were to exist, they may actually be getting the raw end of the deal, although I know that doesn't seem to make sense. After all, obedience and good moods make life so much easier and pleasant, and they won't ever have to deal with getting into trouble. Misconception alert! If children are always obedient and in a good mood, they won't ever test boundaries. That may sound ideal, but without testing boundaries, there would be a lot less learning going on. A child like that may grow up with severe insecurities and not develop a sense of self. They may also grow up to fear making mistakes and disapproval.

While the mythological 'perfect' child doesn't exist, that doesn't mean that you don't come across 'easy' children. These do exist, and may seem perfect because of their calm disposition, confidence, and regular obedience. If your child is one of these 'easy' children, great! If your child isn't an 'easy' child, that's also great! Each child is born with their own unique personality that makes them an individual, different from you or any other person. It's important to understand that just because your child isn't 'easy' doesn't mean that they are bad. There are no bad children. There is only a lack of correct discipline to help them develop and grow properly.

Toddlers Testing the Limits

Think of testing behaviors as a request for a need to be met. When you don't answer that request properly, your child is going to continue to ask over and over again until they get an answer.

If discipline enforcement is left up in the air, it is uncomfortable for both the child and the caregiver. Children are perceptive, and testing toddlers are aware that their behavior is generating a negative emotion within you. Likewise, when you leave a testing toddler hanging without a direct and calm response, you are going to suffer negative consequences as well. You may end up losing your temper or even resenting your child. In severe cases, your child may grow to resent you, and you may lose their affection.

It's healthy and natural for children to test limits. It is your job to make sure that you react immediately, appropriately, and definitively. If you do not react in a definitive way that lets your child know, without a shadow of a doubt, that the behavior is unacceptable and won't be tolerated, they will become locked in limbo. They will get stuck in a testing rut where all they are doing is testing limits instead of fulfilling their potential through learning and growing.

Why Toddlers Test

Toddlers are not adults. Yes, that's stating the obvious, but sometimes we overlook that fact. As adults, we can forget or overlook the fact that toddlers don't have the same impulse and emotional control to express themselves in a way that adults condone as appropriate. It may not be much of a consolation, but your toddler probably doesn't understand their behavior either. They are acting on impulse; they have not spent time developing a carefully laid out plan to undermine your authority and provoke your ire.

The explanation for testing limitations is pretty simple and rooted in your child's biology. They are toddlers; they haven't physically developed the maturity of adults. As such, their brains haven't fully developed and aren't capable of functioning as the brain of an adult. Children have an immature prefrontal cortex. This part of the brain is responsible for making decisions, expressing personality, cognitive behavior, and keeping social behavior in check. Simply put, your child's brain isn't developed enough to handle their turbulent emotions and impulses. As they grow and learn, so does this part of their brain.

Your toddler may register that you are not happy about their behavior, but their impulses in reaction to emotions or stimuli override their brain. The number one rule for effectively dealing with your child acting out is this: don't take it personally. Keep reminding yourself that your child loves you, appreciates you, and needs you more than they even realize. It is important to respect your child by understanding the stage of development they are in, and that limit testing is natural and a crucial part of learning. See it as behavior that is appropriate for their age, and don't react to it as if they have the same cognitive capabilities of adults.

Testing Toddler Tips

Here are some tips to help you stay sane when dealing with a testing toddler.

Give Them Some Rein

Toddlers are at the age where they start to become more independent and autonomous. This is reflected in their behavior. It's a good idea to sometimes offer your child some autonomy, when it's appropriate. A little bit of safe leeway in some instances may lead to less rebellion over other things. For example, don't give your child the option to take a bath or not, that is non-negotiable. Instead, give them a choice between whether they want a bubble bath or bath toys. They are still going to take a bath, but they exerted some authority by making a smaller decision for themselves.

Prevention Rather Than Cure

Learn to anticipate and prevent episodes of acting out. Toddlers can find it a challenge to cooperate with you at the best of times, so be mindful and make it as easy as possible for them to be well behaved. For instance, don't drag a tired or hungry toddler to the store. You are guaranteeing failure. In a similar vein, it may not be effective to explain to your toddler why they are not allowed to do something. They may simply not see the logic in it. Instead, redirect their attention or provide them with acceptable alternatives. If they won't stop throwing hard items such as cups, eating utensils, or hard toys, for instance, offer them some soft type of ball or other soft objects to throw instead. If they won't stop ruining plants in the yard, try distracting them by going for a walk.

Focus on the Positive

Telling your child not to do something is not always going to work. It's also not always effective to get angry and admonish them; after all, negative attention is still attention. Instead, focus on a positive way of deterring the behavior. As an example, when a child is resting the rule of not sitting on a surface they aren't supposed to, such as a glass coffee table, don't react by saying, "Don't sit on the coffee table!" Rather try asking them to put their feet down. Stay calm. The more emotional your response is, the more likely your child is to keep acting out.

Choose When to React

Choosing when to discipline testing behavior will make your life easier. If the behavior isn't all that important, letting it go could even make your child more cooperative in other situations. If you find that you are constantly battling with your child over every little thing, it may be time to take stock and change the rules.

How to Handle Toddler Testing

- Express the limit clearly; don't be vague or unsure, e.g., "You must not make a noise while I am on the telephone."
- Acknowledge your child's feelings or desires, e.g., "I know you want my attention, and that you find it hard to stay quiet while I am focusing on talking on the telephone."
- Be ready to react when testing behavior occurs, e.g., "You are going to wait outside the room until I have finished talking on the telephone. I will give you attention in a few minutes." You should not reiterate the limit a second time. If you are, then you are probably waiting too long between setting the limit and reacting to the testing behavior.
- Accept the fact that there will be a negative response to disciplining testing behavior, and stay calm and level-headed.
- After the discipline, reconnect with your child by acknowledging their feelings and desires again and offering affection.

Get to Know Your Child

Each child has their own personality, unique to them; however, there are certain traits that can be used as a rule of thumb, which may help you understand your child a little better. Understanding your child's general traits can help you to decide on how to discipline them and how to anticipate their acting out behavior.

The temperament of your child points to their individual personality traits. Your child may not fit neatly into one of the categories, but even knowing the categories will help you deal with your child better. There is a certain amount of nature versus nurture, but generally there are certain traits that are common and relatable. There are nine different categories (Rymanowicz, 2017):

- Biological rhythms
- Activity level
- Sensitivity
- Reaction intensity
- Approach/withdrawal
- Adaptability
- Distractibility
- Persistence
- Mood

Even though each person, and each child, has similar traits to another person, they still have a unique combination of traits. You have to understand that there is no right or wrong here, only common traits. Their personality traits give you context and understanding of your child's behavior and how they handle different situations. Understanding their personality traits helps you decide how to react to their behavior. It will also influence your expectations of your child's behavior and help you discipline accordingly.

Biological Rhythms

This refers to someone's regularity of internal drives such as sleeping and eating. Some children have regular rhythms where their biological functions are predictable and regular. They get hungry, want to sleep, or use the toilet at the same time each day. This does help you create a regular routine for your child and help them stick to a more regular routine.

Activity Level

The activity level of your child points to how physically active they are. Some children need more activity and will have a higher energy level versus a child who has a lower activity level who enjoys less active and calmer activities.

High activity level children have the potential to switch between activities quickly. They may be seen as rowdy, boisterous, or disruptive. Slow activities may cause them to become fidgety and they may have difficulty sitting still. Children with a high activity level need to move and run around to burn off their energy. If they have to sit still, make sure to offer them opportunities for quick bursts of energy release such as a quick run around at a rest stop on a long car trip.

Low activity level children are drawn towards calmer and quieter activities, these children may have a propensity to sit still for longer and may appear to have a lower energy level. Offer children with lower activity levels quieter activities to occupy themselves with such as reading.

Sensitivity

How sensitive your child is will determine the intensity of their reactions to even small, seemingly unimportant, stimuli.

Sensitive children will have a more intense reaction to stimuli such as touch, smell, and light. Little things you may not even notice might bother them, such as the feeling of clothing tags. Preempt your child's intense reactions by discovering what they are and aren't comfortable with and trying to accommodate them. You might need to accommodate their sensitivity in various ways, like taking them shopping with you to find clothes they are comfortable in, or offering them a quiet space at a gathering.

Subtle stimuli doesn't bother children with low sensitivity; they may not even react to falling and hurting themselves. These children may require you to be more aware, as their reactions to negative experiences—such as being hurt or sick—may not reflect the true nature of the problem.

Reaction Intensity

Different children react differently to situations. Some react mildly, while others react more strongly. Individuals differ in how strongly they react to situations whether they are positive or negative.

High-intensity children may react strongly to situations, even if the situation isn't a big deal. An example is if your child wants to wear a specific outfit, but it's in the washer, there may be a powerful outburst. Even positive stimuli, such as good news, may be met with intense reactions that could be seen as dramatic. Keep in mind that they are not doing so on purpose; it's a part of their temperament. You will need to teach your high-intensity child more appropriate expressions of their intense feelings.

Low-intensity children may not react to milder situations at all, and their reaction to something that is a big deal may seem lackluster, making it more difficult to pick up on what they are feeling. Realizing that you have a low-intensity child will help you be aware and pick up on subtle emotional expression cues you may have previously missed. You may even need to ask them how they are feeling at times.

Approach/Withdrawal

How easily and quickly your child adjusts to situations is called approach and withdrawal.

Children with an approaching temperament are willing to try new things and meet new people, and may even rush into a situation without hesitation. Providing your child with new and exciting opportunities to explore and meet new people will help encourage their approaching nature.

Children with a withdrawing temperament are often slow to warm up to new people and situations. They may seem more cautious, and they will take more time to become comfortable. These children need to be treated with care and understanding of their temperament, and you need to employ patience and let them take their time to adjust.

Adaptability

How easily a child adapts to change is called adaptability.

Highly adaptable children will adapt easily to sudden changes, even without warning, and may switch quickly from one activity to another without any fuss.

Slow adaptability children don't react well to sudden changes, and may need time and forewarning of any impending changes to their regular routine. They may not transition from one activity to the next well, and may kick up a fuss even transitioning from playtime to lunchtime. You may need to warn them before a switch from even seemingly mundane activities, as they react better when they know changes are coming.

Distractibility

Distractibility has to do with how easily your child is distracted by environmental stimuli, such as sound or other people.

Highly distractible children are quick to move their attention from one thing to the next, these children may find it difficult to focus, especially in environments that are busy with sound, light, colors, movement, etc. They may need your help to focus on a task, and you may need to find them a quiet space or remove distractions when they need to pay attention to important activities, such as homework.

Children with low distractibility are able to focus, sometimes intensely, on tasks even if there is noise, movement, or any potential distractions around them. Because they are not easily distracted, these children may have difficulty overcoming an upset because they focus on their emotions. They need support to help overcome intense emotions.

Persistence

How long you are able and willing to give a task your all is known as persistence.

Children with high persistence may keep trying to master a skill or complete a task irrespective of how challenging it is and how many times they fail before getting it right. These children are more likely to be independent and able to work on an activity without help.

Low persistence children may not want to keep at it when learning a new skill or completing a task, and may feel overwhelmed when they struggle. If they perceive something as difficult, they may want to quickly move on to something else. You may need to help your child and encourage them to keep at it.

Mood

The mood is all about the general attitude with which you handle your feelings and behaviors.

Naturally positive children generally appear happy and optimistic most of the time. They find it easier to move on from negative experiences.

Children who display a more negative mood naturally may appear to be subdued rather than happy most of the time. They may display a calmer, but more negative, attitude toward situations and may not be able to move on from upsetting experiences quickly. You may not pick up on positive feelings from a negative mood child, even though they still feel positivity.

Managing Your Expectations

Understanding your child's temperament will help you have appropriate expectations for them, such as not expecting a toddler who doesn't warm up to others easily to jump at the chance to mingle with their peers. Nor would you expect a toddler to have patience and wait around getting bored. It's not fair on your toddler either way, because those are your expectations as an adult and not age-appropriate expectations for a toddler. Just like it's not fair to expect a toddler to wait patiently, it's not fair to expect a child who is "slow to warm up" to jump into a new playgroup right away. Children with irregular rhythms will require varying routines, while children with low adaptability need stability and regularity. Structuring your daily routine and adapting your expectations according to your child's temperament will help reduce conflict and stress for both you and your child.

Misbehavior or Just Behavior?

Understanding your child's behavior is key to learning how to effectively work with and aid in their development as they grow and learn. You will perceive defiant behavior differently as your child struggles with acquiring some autonomy. You begin to understand that not listening to you can be a result of overwhelming developmental needs. Finding appropriate solutions to developmental behavior will require firmness, in addition to kindness, and will draw on your ability to solve problems. Punishments and lectures may not work, and you may need to find a way around them. It's not necessarily misbehavior once you understand your child; it's just natural behavior as your child develops and grows.

Most of the temperament traits discussed above are what is known as 'average' temperaments. They are generally divided into two categories: inhibited temperament and uninhibited temperament. What if I told you that recently a third temperament has been discovered, referred to as strong-willed? These children actively seek out new and exciting environments and situations instead of simply reacting to the environment they are in.

Tips for Understanding Strong-Willed Children

Understanding your strong-willed child is the most important step to positively molding their behavior!

Gentle Playfulness

You can help your exuberant child develop better self-regulation by using gentle discipline instead of harshness. Instead of reprimanding, try using hints, suggestions, and playful comments. Try using fun activities, like games, to encourage your child to practice self-regulation. They will most likely jump at the opportunity to join in. For example, getting them out the door on time may be more effective by turning it into a game. Playful parenting will serve you well when raising an exuberant child.

Find Positivity

Often the focus falls on exuberant children's intensity, stubbornness, and strong will instead of appreciating the positive aspects. Instead of focusing on the negatives of their personality, focus on the positives, such as their enthusiasm and their ability to be entertaining.They may be impulsive, but they are also cheerful, entertaining, and enthusiastic! The expectations we place on exuberant children stem from the labels we give them; single-minded, stubborn, demanding, defiant. Changing those labels will help you understand and view your child differently.

- A demanding child can be seen as one with leadership skills.
- A defiant child can be seen as one with a strong sense of independence.
- A stubborn child may be seen as having a strong sense of persistence.

- A child who is often negatively viewed as single minded can be seen as having the ability to focus well. (Soderlund, n.d.)

Changing the label from negative to positive will change the way you perceive your child, and you will start to see them in a more positive light.

They Are Just Wired That Way

Temperament is not something that is within a child's control; it's how they are wired. These strong-willed children are described as being exuberant in attaining their goals, even with little things. They actively approach or seek out new experiences and people. Exploration of their world comes naturally to them, and they enjoy it! These children are generally quite positive, very social, and welcome new experiences.

As the parent of a strong-willed child, you need to understand that their exuberance is associated with brain activity in the left frontal lobe. Their brain is literally wired that way; nothing can change their brain chemistry, but you can change your expectations of them.

Common Problems With Discipline Problems and How to Solve Them

Discipline is effective in improving behavior, but is most effective if a supportive environment is provided, positive reinforcement is employed, and you use suitable strategies for your reactions. However, before you can start correcting undesirable behavior, you need to understand the cause.

Bossiness

Naturally dominant personalities are a natural part of life. However, allowing a dominant child to be overly bossy sets a precedent for unacceptable bossiness. Children may not have developed the ability to differentiate between bossy, and decisive but polite communication. Teach your child to be more cooperative, and teach them better phrasing of their demands. Turn "We are going to do this now." into "Would you like to do this?"

Note: Children copycat behavior, so it's important that you don't bark orders, so that you model respectful communication.

Biting

Biting is a common form of communication used to express feelings when children haven't developed expressive language skills yet. Often it's used to express frustration, rather than aggression with intent to cause harm.

Verbally expressing the pain and moving away from the biter, while firmly expressing that it is not an acceptable behavior, sends a clear message. Tending to whoever was bitten and not providing the biter with attention reinforces the message that biting will not garner attention. Encourage an apology and offer examples of positive physical contact, such as hugging, to demonstrate the difference between which forms of communication are acceptable, and which are not. If your child is a regular biter, be aware of triggers. When visible triggers—such as frustration—are observed, encourage acceptable verbal expressions of feelings.

Lying

There is often a reason behind a child telling lies. Many times the reason for lying is because a child is afraid of being punished. Similarly, children may fear rejection from a caregiver if they were to tell the truth. Sometimes children will also lie if they are being threatened, or backed into a corner they cannot escape from. Finding the cause of the habit helps prevent it. Express that it doesn't sound like the truth and encourage the truth to be told. Think about your typical reaction to mistakes and adjust them, if need be, in order to ensure that the correct message is sent: it's okay to be imperfect. When your child tells the truth, acknowledge it by thanking them, even when it's difficult to do so.

Note: Distinguish between outright lying and fabricating tall tales. Telling tales, such as seeing a dinosaur, expresses your child's imagination and shouldn't be discouraged.

Hitting and Kicking

Again, this is usually an expression of overwhelming feelings, such as anger or frustration. The steps to correct the behavior are similar to those for biting. Immediate intervention to stop the behavior is required, and you must provide an explanation that feelings are valid, but physically lashing out is not. Again, encourage the use of appropriate verbal expression and redirect the behavior to a more positive expression, such as hitting a pillow instead.

Note: Hitting your child, for whatever reason, as a form of discipline reinforces the idea that it is acceptable behavior.

Tattling

A regular struggle for children is being able to establish boundaries. They don't possess the necessary skills to work conflicts out themselves without your help. Tattling, such as "I was playing with it first!" is an opportunity for you to teach your child how to resolve and manage conflicts. Turn the focus from the other person's behavior onto your child's own feelings by asking them how being treated like that made them feel. Teach your child effective verbal communication to express themselves when they don't like how others treat them. Learning to resolve conflict and establish boundaries is vital in developing confidence and assertiveness.

Back-Talking

Talking back may seem to develop before other expressive language skills, with 'no' being one of the first words that children learn. Parents may expect opposition to their requests, but it's often the tone used by your child that will be the most upsetting for you. Immediately address the behavior when it happens. Offer your child a second chance to comply before you enforce a consequence, such as, "Let's try that again." If the behavior persists, then it's time to use appropriate discipline to discourage future back-talking.

Temper Tantrums

Young children are often frustrated when they find themselves in between their dependence on you and gaining their independence. Temper tantrums may be seen as an expression of a failed attempt to control the situation. Again, your child may not have the necessary language skills to express themselves, and then react to overwhelming emotion with a tantrum. These outbursts and loss of control over their emotions may even be scary for the child. As the parent, instead of losing your temper yourself, provide a soothing presence for your child. Sometimes it helps to remove the child from the situation to help them regain composure. Don't give in to their demands, as this encourages the behavior as a means of getting what they want. Instead, help your child to find the words that will allow them to express their feelings.

Whining

Whining is a common behavior among children, and is usually an indication that they want attention if they feel unimportant or ignored. It may also be an expression of fatigue, hunger, or frustration. You may be tempted to ignore the whining to get the message across that it isn't working; however, offering your child a hug may be more effective. Physical affection and positive attention often resolve the issue. You can also try lifting your child's mood by offering them a few minutes of physical play at regular intervals.

Interrupting

When your attention is directed at someone else, your child may feel that their importance is being threatened and may demand immediate attention as a result. Instead of harshly admonishing your child for the interruption, forewarn them when your attention is going to be directed elsewhere. Redirect your child's attention to an activity that will occupy them, to help them deal with that lack of attention. Tell them that they will have your attention after you have finished a phone call or visiting a friend, to send them a clear message that you have enough attention to go around. Then, follow through on that promise.

Note: Teach your child to recognize pauses in conversation and to appropriately interrupt with "excuse me" if it's an emergency.

Conflicts Between Siblings

Sibling conflict is not a new occurrence. Children generally don't like it when they don't get their way, and if two or more children are of this opinion and in the same space, conflicts are bound to arise. Similarly to how tattling can be managed, teaching children how to verbally express their feelings can help them learn how to handle and resolve conflicts. Help your child see things from their sibling's point of view while reassuring them that their feelings are valid. Don't focus on the conflict by only intervening when conflict arises. You should also offer positive feedback when they get along well.

Note: Prevent sibling rivalry by not making comparisons, as well as acknowledging each child's unique abilities and expressing their individual value equally.

Arguments

Power struggles are common with strong-willed children. They just don't give up when they are in disagreement with you. Don't engage in or entertain arguments. Offer a simple warning that if the arguing continues then a consequence will follow. Engaging in a power struggle with your child isn't going to get anybody anywhere. You are the adult, and your child must learn to fall in line with what you tell them to do, without argument.

But Why?

Strong-willed children may demand to know why a limitation is being imposed. "Because I said so," is often the most frustrating response for your child to hear. If they do not see the logic behind the limitation, they are likely to continue to misbehave. Offer them a brief and clear explanation; resist the temptation to lecture them.

Refusal to Comply

Children will often refuse to do what they don't want to do, especially if they are strong-willed. A simple possible solution is to offer them a choice. Turn, "Pack your toys away now," into, "You can pack your toys away now, or in 10 minutes." You are not offering them the choice to do it or not, but simply having a choice to do it now or in 10 minutes can make them feel empowered.

Making Their Own Rules

You will find that your child doesn't want to comply with your rules, but instead they want to make up their own to suit themselves. Don't entertain power struggles and arguing and don't overwhelm your child with too many rules or orders. Enforce consequences for important rules that need to be followed, but allow natural consequences to occur for minor issues. For example, If your child refuses to wear shoes when going outside, then the natural consequence is that their feet may hurt on hot tar or over stones. This will encourage them to listen to you in the future.

Impatience

Strong-willed children are not likely to want to wait for anything; however, waiting is an inevitable part of life. In instances where you know there is going to be waiting, make it clear to your child that if they don't like waiting, they have the option to bring something along to entertain themselves, or wait and be bored. Give them options and allow them to choose how they entertain themselves while waiting.

Want vs. Need

Children will often insist that they need something when they actually just want it because they aren't able to distinguish the difference. They may still feel upset even if they get what they want because, in their opinion, they aren't getting their fair share. Fairness is a big concern for children. Try employing a token economy system, which is a reward system where good behavior rewards your child with what they want so, that they don't feel as though they are being punished for bad behavior. For example, cleaning their room earns them TV time. Not cleaning their room means they didn't earn that TV time.

Setting Their Own Pace

Children are famous for moving fast for something they want to do, and procrastinating when they don't want to do it. Again, just as with ignoring you, give an order and a consequence, and immediately enforce the consequence if they dawdle.

Ignoring You

Strong-willed children are extremely good at employing selective hearing. They simply ignore what they don't want to hear. It's tempting to employ punishments for this behavior, but that isn't going to help much. If you set a limit or give an order, offer a consequence. If you are ignored, immediately address being ignored and follow through with the consequence to let your child know that you aren't just doling out idle threats.

Consistency Is Key

Consistently and immediately correcting an undesirable behavior will quickly reaffirm the message of your authority. Inconsistency and delayed responses to misbehavior can become confusing and impede the development of more acceptable behaviors.

Positives of a Strong-Willed Child

Having a strong-willed child isn't all doom and gloom! There are many positives to look at and appreciate, such as the following (Wolff, 2016):

- A study conducted over 40 years and published in Developmental Psychology revealed that children who break the rules are likely to become high-income earners in the future.
- Strong-willed children often make great leaders who don't shy away from standing up for what they believe in.
- They think outside the box and possess incredible creativity.
- They enjoy discovering things for themselves instead of being sheep-like and just accepting things at face value.
- They have unshakable determination to reach their goals in life, which often leads to success.
- They make really good debaters because they question everything and aren't afraid to argue their point.
- Strong-willed children have the ability to influence those around them to get what they want, a great quality to have for later on in life.
- They are passionate about life and everything they do which they do with admirable enthusiasm.

Okay, enough about why being a strong-willed child is great for them; what about you? What benefits do you get out of having a strong-willed child?

- They can be exhausting at the best of times, which means you need to up your self-care. Whether it's getting fitter from running after them, or taking extra time out for yourself, looking after yourself better can never be a bad thing.
- Strong-willed children make you think. They might be questioning the world around them, or they may be giving you a reason to reflect on your own actions and thoughts.
- They humble you. You might have had the notion that you would be the perfect parent before your strong-willed child came along and completely altered that sense of ego. They also remind you that you are only human.
- Their iron will teach you to have an even stronger one. This helps you feel less intimidated by situations that may have overwhelmed you in the past.

A Word of Encouragement

As the parent of a strong-willed child, it's easy to sink into a pit of feeling alone in your struggles when you see other children who don't test their parents as much. One of the first important things you need to understand and remind yourself of is that you are not alone. Strong-willed children are not uncommon, and there are many parents out there who are going through the same daily battles.

Always keep in mind that your exuberant child is unique; you created a one-of-a-kind little individual! There is not another child out there who is exactly the same as yours.

Don't isolate yourself. Building a strong support system to help you through trying times will go a long way to keeping you sane. Even just talking to someone about what you are feeling can lighten your load considerably. You can find other parents of strong-willed children to build friendships with which will make you feel less alone.

The toddler and young child phases of strong-willed children don't last forever. As your child grows, develops, and begins to mature emotionally, your struggles won't be in vain. Many strong-willed children do eventually come to see their parents' point of view and become easier to handle.

Develop an attitude that is patient, calm, and don't sweat the small things. Be compassionate and sensitive. Compassion can help you overcome obstacles faced when you have a strong-willed child. When you show them compassion, understanding, and empathy they will be more likely to respond positively.

Foster courage in yourself; your job as the parent of an exuberant child is important, and things will ultimately become easier and better over time. Take time for yourself so that you can offer your child your best, and reach out to others to maintain your sanity. You're doing a great job already, because you love your child enough to seek out knowledge to better understand them and overcome the obstacles you both face.

Chapter 2:

Discipline the Healthy Way

The goal parents instinctively strive for is to be the best parents possible. Parents want to provide a nurturing environment for their child, and to handle any conflict in such a way that it has a positive outcome. When you have a strong-willed child who misbehaves, acts out, and is stubborn, you need to guide that child with positive discipline. This is a powerful tool for all parents, and it will strengthen the bond between parent and child without breaking down the relationship. Healthy discipline is based on respect, love, and understanding from both sides, and it benefits parents and children. Using healthy discipline makes it possible for a strong-willed child to learn to regulate their temperament and reactions.

Classical Conditioning vs. Non-Punitive Parenting

People endlessly debate on whether your own childhood shapes and influences what your own parenting skills will be. Some disagree vehemently on this and insist we cannot blame our own childhood lessons and influences on how we discipline our children. Many feel that parents are adults and should base their actions only on logic that is not influenced by outside factors; however, everything about ourselves plays a role in how we approach parenting. But we have the ability to acknowledge this, learn from it, and be able to guide our children through positive discipline.

Why Some Parents Don't Accept Non-Punitive Methods

We learned discipline from our parents and the way they handled and applied discipline throughout our own childhoods. Whether their way was good or not, that is what each of us was exposed to, and we absorbed that.

Assumptions are another facet of how we see discipline. We assumed that what we were taught is the best and only way, and we often automatically fall back on those assumptions without logically thinking it through.

Ethnicity and culture can also play a huge role in how we approach discipline. Certain cultures have functioned using authoritarian discipline for countless centuries. As young parents, it is often not easy to go against the norm of what is acceptable within the culture. This is why using positive, healthy discipline will make an incredible difference in your strong-willed child's life: you are also laying the foundation for your child to one day use healthy and positive discipline when they become parents themselves.

Society is another culprit that brings great pressure on parents to conform to societal norms. In addition, people often speak of discipline when they actually mean punishment. They see it as the same thing; discipline for many must be applied through punishing a child, and that is the only way children learn. Many people still believe in the concept of 'punishment for sins or trespasses' and that children should suffer in small ways for what they did, or they will not learn to behave.

What is Non-Punitive Parenting?

Non-punitive parenting means moving away from the accepted norms of punishment, such as spanking, taking away 'privileges', time-outs, and withholding affection to show a child how much the parent disapproves of their behavior. Punitive parenting is a cycle of punishment, angry yelling, often shaming the child—even in public—and "awarding" a child (in plain language—bribing the child) for what the parent considers to be good behavior and to encourage them to keep behaving well.

Non-punitive discipline turns all the old norms completely around; there are no threats of punishment, and no bribes to entice them to behave well. Healthy discipline is based on respect for yourself, respect for your child, and gaining the respect and trust of your child.

It is important that parents understand and accept that not punishing a child does not mean the child grows up as a hooligan with no discipline. Bad and unacceptable behavior does have consequences. Non-punitive discipline is not being a permissive parent at all! You will set boundaries and rules; you are simply changing the consequences of a specific behavior of your child.

Non-violent communication replaces the arguments and yelling and fear of being punished physically. Instead, you guide your child to learn that when their behavior is out of control, they will be removed from the situation until they can control themselves. If they cannot play with a toy without throwing it around or trying to break it, the toy will be removed.

Positive Discipline in a Nutshell

Discipline is teaching your child what is and isn't acceptable. When you use positive discipline instead of punitive discipline, you are teaching and guiding your strong-willed child in the most loving way a parent possibly can. You're teaching them how to regain control of their emotions, how to behave acceptably, and how to respect themselves and others.

Positive discipline is not confined to a specific age or environment. It can be used effectively from the toddler stage, throughout childhood, and even in the teenage years! It is also not only confined to the home; it works effectively for teachers in the classroom and all caregivers who interact with children. Positive discipline employed in all these areas ensures the maximum opportunity for children to learn from their mistakes and blunders.

How Do We Define Positive Discipline?

The following defines what makes discipline positive, how it is in contrast with negative discipline (punishment):

Solving Problems Together

When problems arise, sit your child down and discuss the problem with them. Ask questions that will lead to your child giving input. Problem-solving skills are a very important skill for every child to learn, and you start the process. Ask simple questions, such as, "You have not packed your toys away for two days. What do you think we can do about this?"

Remember that mutual respect is critically important in problem-solving with your child, so never ask questions that would be perceived as an attack or accusations. You should use this as an opportunity for your child to share their opinions and solutions to a specific problem. When your child is given the opportunity to come up with a solution, they feel empowered and tend to be eager to cooperate.

Discipline Instead of Punishment

Punishment is the exact opposite of teaching your child consequences, and showing your child that negative behavior comes with consequences teaches them valuable life lessons. You prepare your child for adulthood, where consequences can have a huge impact on their lives. So, positive discipline teaches them how to become responsible adults.

Teaching Is the Focus

When you make teaching the focus of discipline, it does away with misunderstandings and confusion for children. Use clear instructions, explain what the expectations are, and physically guide them.

For example, when you want them to do chores, actually show them how they should make their beds, or how to use an appliance, such as the vacuum cleaner. Sit with them and show them how to fold their clothes to pack it away, and you turn the lesson into together-time as well.

Encouragement, Not Praise

Praising children constantly for things they accomplish gives them a false sense of their self-worth and does not teach them how to handle failure. Focus instead on encouragement when they struggle to achieve success or find it difficult to master a skill.

Encouragement makes your child feel that you love and appreciate them, even when they do not succeed or struggle to succeed. It also deepens their sense of belonging. In turn, this gives them the motivation to strive and learn to be independent, as they want to achieve things on their own.

Parents, you must always remember that you are the model to your children, and they will handle failure how they see you deal with it. Always make sure you apologize to your child when you mess up. This is an incredibly important life lesson in positive discipline for your child! It helps reinforce the fact that mistakes are made by everyone, and mistakes don't make a person unlovable.

Positive Relationship Building

It is important for parents to spend quality time each day with their children. This might seem like a side-step away from the concept of discipline but in reality, it is an important aspect of positive discipline.

You should make time in your day to play with your child, or have time together just to chat. Spending quality time with a child builds a strong, positive relationship between parent and child.

Encourage your child to tell you about his or her day, and ask questions like, "When did you feel happy today? Was there a time you felt sad or angry?" When you discuss feelings with your child, they learn to open up about their emotions and this builds deep trust.

Parents should take this opportunity to tell their children about their own day, and what their feelings were at different times during this day. This quality time is a golden opportunity for both parents and children as you learn more about each other in a relaxed, non-confrontational setting. Each time you spend quality time with your child in this way, you build strong foundations for a strong parent-child relationship that will be healthy and keep growing over time.

Positive and Effective Discipline Strategies

When you use positive discipline strategies, you remove the age-old battle between children and parents. Punitive discipline always leads to threats, physical punishment, bribing children to behave, yelling, and arguments that never really solve any problems.

The following strategies have proven to be effective with strong-willed children and contribute greatly to harmonious family life.

Time-In vs. Time-Out

Time-out can be used effectively for discipline as a consequence. Unfortunately, parents can tend to use it too often, or as the only option to remove a child from a situation or when misbehaving.

Instead of sending a child to time-out alone, make this a time-in where you sit down with your child. Read a book with your little one and, if possible, make it interactive. This works wonderfully when the child needs to calm down and focus on something other than the situation that caused the problem. Time-in can also be used for stubborn children who do not want to apologize for their behavior. But make sure that your child is aware that he or she will not return to a previous activity until they apologize for their behavior.

Positive Attention and Reinforcement

Give your child positive reinforcement when they do the right thing! Praise them for sharing toys, or being kind to another person. Tell them that you are proud of their generosity. Children need this balance, instead of only getting attention when they have broken the rules.

Simple, Single-Word Prompts

Instead of harsh demands such as, "Stop running and go put your toys away!", use a casual, gentle tone and give simple reminders like, "Walk. Toys." Children are less likely to become defensive when you use gentle one-word reminders. This also shows a child who acts out to get negative attention that that behavior will not work, and you are not going to lose your temper.

Redirection

Children have short attention spans, and this works in your favor when they are acting out. It is easy to redirect them when you offer them another activity. You can offer a different toy and, if the child still acts out, take them to another room in the house, or take them outside and offer an outdoor activity. This strategy works for older children as well, by offering an age-appropriate activity instead of saying he has to stop playing computer games. Positive redirection de-escalates situations, and there will be less defiance and arguments.

Set Up Family Rules

Setting up family rules need not be a dreaded task that complicates your life! Keep to the following guidelines, and you will be able to set up family rules that will be easy for everyone to keep to.

- Be specific, clear, and simple so that your child understands them.
- Make them age-appropriate and achievable so that your child can easily comply.
- Be consistent in enforcing the same rules all the time.

- Both parents must collaborate and mutually agree on the rules to ensure overall consistency.

Why Should Negative Discipline Be Avoided?

Parents normally do not set out with the goal to apply negative discipline on purpose. They may fall into this habit when they are stressed, or perhaps they find parenthood taxing without realizing the harm they do. Negative discipline can often work short-term, but for all the wrong reasons. The long-term harm far outweighs the short-term benefits; negative discipline can have a devastating impact on the mental and emotional development of a child.

What Forms Does Negative Discipline Take?

- Spanking.
- Shaking a baby or toddler in a fit of temper, or in frustration.
- Smacking their fingers with your hand, a ruler, or any similar object.
- Yelling at your child.
- Putting a guild trip on a child.
- Subjecting a child to the silent treatment.
- Threats of leaving, even if you would never do that.
- Threats to deprive your child of necessities such as water, sleep, or food.
- Unrealistic expectations.
- Shaming.
- Name-calling.

- Sarcasm.
- Belittling remarks and looks.
- Teasing in a negative and belittling manner.

Right and Wrong Questions Parents Ask

Parents who are determined to use punishment as the form of discipline they prefer often ask the wrong questions when asking for advice, such as:

- How do I make my child do as I tell them to do?
- How do I actually get my child to listen to what I tell them?
- How do I make my child understand the meaning of "no"?
- How do I make this problem go away and never come back?

The above questions are completely opposite to the questions that parents who want to build loving parent-child relationships ask! The questions positive discipline parents ask address the bigger picture, and they're thinking of the long-term consequences and benefits for the future. They ask:

- How do I help my child learn problem-solving skills, cooperation, and respect?
- How do I help my child feel a sense of significance, self-worth, and belonging?
- How do I help my child feel empowered and capable?
- How do I turn problems into opportunities for learning for myself and my child?
- How do I get into my child's world and understand the process of his mental, emotional, and physical development?

It is often quite an eye-opener for parents when they read through the questions above; they often learn things about themselves that they may not be comfortable with. These questions are guidelines for parents who realize that they need to work on their own mindset regarding discipline. They point the way to move away from punitive to positive discipline.

Misbehavior and Consequences

Effective Use of Consequences

- Consequences are used to deter unacceptable behavior.
- Explain the consequences in relation to their actions clearly.
- Provide a warning before enforcing a consequence.
- Choose consequences carefully in advance and make them appropriate.
- Effective consequences needn't be severe or harsh. If they're too harsh, power struggles and resentment may ensue.
- Milder consequences are often more effective.

Examples of Consequences

The following is a list of consequences, their definitions, and how they should be used in order to be the most effective.

Losing Privileges

Losing the opportunity to enjoy activities or ending an activity immediately as a result of misbehavior during the activity can be a highly effective way to discourage said behavior.

- Loss of privileges due to irresponsible behavior teaches your child to be more responsible.
- Enforce the consequence for a specified, but limited, period of time.
- Loss of privileges for an extended period of time often has no more value than for shorter periods.
- Shorter loss of privilege time is often easier to enforce and manage.

Losing a Material Item

Losing the use of a needed (but not essential) item, such as crafting scissors, a favorite toy, or removing points from their reward chart.

This consequence is similar to, and just as effective as, the loss of privileges.

Time-Out

- Use a child's own room or a specified time-out area.
- Don't go over the specified time period for the time-out.
- Use a timer to keep track.
- Time-outs generally last for one minute per year of the child's age.
- Alternative time-outs teach your child that the area is a "feel better" space that they can leave when they feel better, or have decided to behave more appropriately.

Employing Consequences

- Clearly explain the rule. This may need to be reiterated time and time again. This affords your child the chance to avoid the behavior. Explaining the rule several times offers your child the chance to comply without moving to give a warning too quickly.
- Sometimes it's beneficial to offer two choices to get your message across (e.g., your child can choose to either share their toys now, or participate in another activity, other than the one in which they are refusing to share).
- Redirect with acceptable alternatives, like kicking a ball rather than a person.
- Warn your child of the consequence clearly to give them a chance to correct the behavior.
- Warn them of the impending consequence only once.
- If they continue the behavior despite the warning, enforce the consequence immediately.
- What to remember:
  - Be brief and clear about the rules and consequences.
  - Only state the rule and consequence when the behavior reflects the need to do so.
  - Ignore any complaints from your child.
  - Only discuss the rule and consequence after the consequence has been enforced and emotions have calmed.
  - Distracting your child may be effective instead of employing a consequence and allow them to shift their focus to more positive behavior.
  - Anticipate misbehavior in order to avoid it.

Discussing Rules and Consequences

- Discuss the details or rules and consequences at a different time to the misbehavior taking place.
- Provide reasons for the rule.
- Acknowledge your child's emotions and desires at the time of the misbehavior.
- Use "I" statements when explaining your point of view and resulting feelings.
- Explain the natural bed consequences of their behavior (e.g., if you skate in the road, you may be run over by a car and then you could not skate anymore because you got hurt).
- Express how their misbehavior affects others in a negative way.
- Help your child to find appropriate alternatives for their misbehavior, such as punching a pillow instead of someone else, or putting their dirty clothes into the laundry basket so they don't have such a large pile to clean up as a consequence.

Punishment vs. Consequence

- Consequence denotes an appropriate reaction in relation to the misbehavior.
- Punishment denotes a severe reaction to the misbehavior, regardless of how minor it may have been.
- Severe punishment is seen as unacceptable parenting in today's day and age.
- Punishment is often ineffective and teaches children to misbehave and get away with it.

- Harsh punishments include physically harming your child and verbally harming them using methods such as harsh criticism or humiliation. These punishments are considered child abuse.
- Harsh punishment leads to a lack of internalizing values and a lack of development of a healthy conscience.
- Harsh punishments often lead to resentment of the parent by the child, weakening the child-parent bond. With strong-willed children, this is a culprit of further and more intense acting out.
- Severe punishments may lead to fear and anxiety, inhibiting the development of assertiveness, development of self-identity, and healthy self-expression.

Building Blocks of Positive Discipline

Positive discipline is based on a set of criteria or building blocks which, when put together, form a solid foundation for disciplining your child the right way.

The Five Criteria of Positive Discipline

- It is efficient over the long-term whereas punishment is a short-term solution that carries lasting negative effects.
- It is kind, yet firm, which equates to being respectful and encouraging toward your child.
- It connects you with your child by providing them with a sense that they are significant and that they belong.
- It offers children opportunities to realize just how capable they really are and how to utilize their full potential constructively.
- It teaches your child invaluable social skills and general life skills, such as concern for others, contribution, accountability,

problem-solving, respect, and cooperation. These help to build a good character within your child.

Positive Discipline Tools and Concepts

Mutual respect is shown when a parent models good character for their child by respecting not only themselves, but also the needs of each particular situation. They model kindness for their child when they respect that child's individual needs.

- Using educational discipline that isn't punitive or permissive.
- Employing problem-solving skills and effective communication.
- Focusing on encouragement rather than praise by noticing the effort put in and the improvement made. Focusing on only success doesn't build self-esteem and a sense of empowerment in the long-term.
- Not focusing on punishment, but focusing instead on solutions.
- Recognizing the reason behind the behavior by understanding those reasons and trying to change the belief behind the actions, not just the behavior itself.

Positive Discipline and Intermittent Reinforcement

Continuous reinforcement is when a child's good behavior is praised every time the desired behavior occurs.

Intermittent reinforcement is when good behavior is praised every few times it occurs and the amount of praise varies.

Children on an intermittent reinforcement schedule aren't able to predict when praise will be offered and are likely to continue good behavior in case they get praise. The likelihood that good behavior will continue over the longer-term is increased when you use intermittent reinforcement, as opposed to offering praise every single time the desired behavior occurs. ("Intermittent," n.d.)

Instructional Responses

When a child misbehaves due to a misunderstanding of the rules or values, an instructional response is required. You need to explain it to them again, ensure that they understand, and offer them another chance to obey the rule.

Make it clear to your child that <u>they</u> are being given an instruction, and <u>they</u> are expected to do it, not anybody else.

Be Specific

State the instruction positively and be specific.

What not to do: "Stop playing." This instruction is phrased negatively and is sending your child the wrong message. You don't want them to stop coloring indefinitely; you just want them to put their crayons away for now.

What to do: "Alice, please put your toys away." There is no negative connotation and the instruction is specific to the desired action.

Instruct, not Request

Don't make the instruction a request (e.g., "Could you put your toys away now?"), and don't leave confusion about who the instruction is for (e.g., "Let's put the crayons away now."). Instructions that begin with 'we' or 'let's' create confusion as to who the instruction is for, and also give the impression that there is a choice whether to obey.

What to say: "John, please put the trains away now." This instruction applies specifically to your child and states one clear task.

Neutrality

Give instructions in a calm and neutral tone.

After giving an instruction, remain silent, watch, and wait. If you walk away without watching and waiting for the instruction to be obeyed, your child may think it's optional. If after some waiting the instruction hasn't been obeyed, repeat it, and give a warning of impending consequence.

One At a Time

Instructions should encompass only one task at a time. If mult-part instructions are given, children may disobey unintentionally due to forgetting a step in the instruction.

What not to do: "Peter, please put your airplane away, wash your hands, and set the table."

What to do: Tell your Peter to put the airplane away. Once that has been completed, tell him to wash his hands. After he has finished washing his hands, tell him to set the table.

Correctional Responses

Correctional responses take place when the rule or instruction has been understood, but your child chooses to misbehave anyway. In the case of correctional responses, it is important to state the rule clearly. Provide only one warning of the consequence to follow. Follow through with the consequence.

Principles of Behavioral Correction

Reject the actual action or behavior when your child misbehaves. Never reject the child as a person.

- Always ensure that the correction provided has a clear direction.
- Make sure that all corrections provided are non-judgmental.
- Express your appreciation when your child listens and complies with the correction.

End the correction by reiterating that you expect your child to cooperate after the correction has ended (e.g., "I know you will do better the next time").

Why You Should Never Spank Them

Society as a whole is moving away from corporal punishment, and there is a good reason for it! Corporal punishment may actually make the behavior worse, instead of making it better; physical actions of violence may also have a negative long-term impact on your child.

Corporal punishment makes children more likely to be aggressive and defiant in the future. It shows them that negative physical contact is normal. There are simply no benefits to corporal punishment. (Fox, 2018)

Spanking is considered to be a negative discipline, and children develop better with positive discipline strategies.

Discipline Can Be Challenging

Discipline is a prickly subject for any parent. If you ask anyone with children about their experiences with disciplining their kids, you are sure to hear at least a couple of horror stories. It doesn't have to be that way for you! Understanding your child, building their trust, maintaining open communication, and knowing how to use discipline positively will go a long way towards achieving positive discipline and cooperation from your child. Another aspect that will help to make your job as a disciplinarian easier is the attitude you have towards discipline and your child.

Your Attitude Matters

Your attitude towards your job as a parent, discipline, and even toward your child can make a big difference on whether implementing discipline is easier or more difficult. Always discipline from a place of love and understanding; don't ever discipline from a place of anger or frustration. Discipline with love will always be in the best interest of your child. Discipline from a place of anger can lead to a negative experience, or even negative discipline techniques.

When disciplining your child, it's important to maintain a firm, but not entirely rigid, attitude. The understanding of both your child and positive discipline will give you the insight necessary to be flexible if the situation calls for it. Not every situation will be exactly the same. The reason behind the behavior sometimes needs to be looked at in greater detail so that you can adjust the discipline to meet that underlying need. Being inflexible could result in a negative outcome. Discipline isn't something that can be done 'by the book.' Each child is an individual, and each situation is unique. Don't just dole out consequences without taking a look at and understanding the whole picture. You never know when you may need to adjust your discipline and be flexible to do what's best for your child.

One more thing to be aware of is your perception of your child. Don't allow yourself to become fixated on the problem behavior to the extent that you start to view your child negatively. Viewing your child negatively will lead to having a negative attitude toward them and toward discipline.

Guard Against Developing a Negative Perception

You can easily find yourself sliding down the slippery slope of developing a negative perception of your child. Parenting is a tough job. You are going to experience highs and lows. It's all part of the rollercoaster ride of life and having a strong-willed child. Sometimes we start focusing too much on the behavior itself, and not enough on the child, their emotions, and the reasons behind the behavior. Remember how we've mentioned that the world labels strong-willed children as 'bad children.' When you focus solely on the behavior, it becomes easy to label your child the same way. Your child will quickly and easily pick up on any negative attitude you have toward them, and this will only serve to break down the trusting relationship between you. When there is no trust and a lot of negativity, the problems will only grow and become more frequent. Be sure to guard yourself against developing a negative perception of your child, so that you maintain your calm and positive discipline strategies. Some advice on how to avoid developing negativity toward your child include:

- Don't ever make generalizations about your child. Sweeping generalizations prevent you from seeing each situation clearly. Focus on each specific situation.
- Don't allow your perception of your child to focus on the misbehavior. Keep your eyes open to everything your child does right. Actively seeking out the positives will help you deal with the negatives more easily, as you will realize that your child possesses both negatives and positives, and not just one or the other.

Children act out; they express themselves in ways that aren't appropriate, and they may even say or do things that are hurtful to you. It is vital that you don't take it personally! If they misbehave, it's often an expression or an underlying need, so don't take it personally. If they get angry because they aren't getting their way and they tell you that they don't like you, don't take it personally. They haven't yet developed the emotional maturity to recognize their emotions and react more appropriately. Your child loves you; they just aren't expressing their emotions correctly.

When you are raising a strong-willed child, it's important to have a strong support system in place. You need to be tenacious and keep to your discipline strategies, even if you aren't making progress in leaps and bounds. Any small measure of progress is still progress, and things will get better over time. Don't let yourself fall into a pit of hopelessness or feeling helpless; this will only make you more prone to developing a negative perception of your child.

Tips for Letting Go of Anger

Anger is a natural response to your child's misbehavior or breaking the rules. It's important to acknowledge that it's natural; however, just because it's natural doesn't mean that you can let it consume you and dictate your discipline strategies, your attitude, or your perception of your child. When anger is hanging over you like a shroud, you develop resentment toward your child. When that happens, even the most normal things they do will make you feel grumpy and resentful. Here are a few tips on how to let go of the anger and reconnect:

- Stop and reconnect with the present. Sometimes stressful situations can trigger a fight or flight response. When this response is triggered, it can be difficult to think clearly without feeling overwhelmed or wanting to give up or lash out. When you feel like you have triggered that response, take a moment to reconnect with the present so that you can think clearly.
  - To do this, stop and pick out:
  - Three things that you can see.
  - Three things that you can hear.
  - Three things that you can feel.

    Then repeat the exercise identifying two of each, and then repeat it again identifying one of each. If you need more grounding, repeat the entire exercise from the beginning.

- Let it out. Sometimes just being able to talk honestly to someone who won't be judgemental can do you the world of good. Talk to someone who understands, won't judge, and won't try to offer their personal opinion, but will listen and let you get it all off your chest.
- Remember their age. Sometimes it's easy to forget your child's actual age and expect them to react more like adults. Remind yourself of how old they actually are, and how much less time

they've had to develop than you have. You may just realize that your expectations are just a little too high for your child.

- Be funny. In an intensely emotional moment, such as a tantrum, anger can escalate quickly. At that moment, grab your child's attention by doing something funny. You may try making a silly face, doing a silly dance, or anything else that will distract them and get both of you laughing. As they say, "Laughter is the best medicine."

- Hug it out. When you feel that you are teetering on the edge of emotional collapse, try bringing your child into a big hug and telling them some of the things you love about them. Hugs release feel-good chemicals in the body, and reminding yourself of the good things you love about your child by verbally telling them aloud can help make the anger melt away.

The Risk of Resentment

Many parents fear risking their child's resentment when it comes to disciplining their children. This fear is one of the parenting fears that may lead to overly permissive parenting; however, you cannot let that fear get in the way of responsible parenting. Doing so could prove to be detrimental to your child's health and well-being and your confidence as a parent.

Discipline is never easy. We all want to see our children happy and smiling, and we want them to always see us in a positive light with nothing but unconditional love on their faces. But no job is easy, and parenting is your job; it's the responsibility you owe to your family and to your child. When done right, discipline won't result in resentment. It's important to find that balance between being a warm and loving parent and being a responsible disciplinarian. It doesn't have to be one way or the other. When you create that balance your discipline comes from a place of love and understanding.

Sure, you may sometimes feel like you are being mean. You may even find yourself feeling like a monster for not giving in to your child's demands. They may get angry with you, frustrated, and they may even end up acting out. Nobody likes to be told 'no', least of all a child. Keep in mind that they don't know the difference between want and need, and they don't have a clue what is in their best interest and what is not. The decision is up to you to make. When you make that decision out of love, and with the knowledge that this is the best thing for your child, you need to trust that things will work themselves out.

Keep an honest and open line of communication with your child and nurture a trusting relationship with them. This will make communicating your reasons for discipline easier and your child will eventually come round to the fact that you do actually know better than they do.

Chapter 3:

The Limits of Parental Influence

Parents feel responsible for how their children turn out in life, and what kind of adults they grow up to be. After all, your child is your responsibility until they turn 18. Until they are of age, it's your job to exert your control over them. That control encompasses a wide range of aspects of their lives from their education, their physical and psychological well-being, the foods they eat, and even the clothes they wear. As it turns out, there are many adults who suffer from a variety of problems, including adjustment issues and emotional and psychological issues. A lot of these issues stem back to experiences during their childhood and growing up.

How far does your influence as their parent really go, and how much of their future adulthood do you control while they are growing up under your care?

There are cases in which adults are well adjusted, but came from family backgrounds that were less than ideal. There are those who came from good family backgrounds and were raised by exemplary parents who ended up going astray as teenagers and adults. Some are from good families and turn out well, and some are from less than ideal families and turn out poorly. Some make it into adulthood without issues, and some develop psychological problems, such as depression. The many variables that may contribute to how your child turns out may lead you to ask the question, "Are parents to blame if their child doesn't end up as a well-adjusted adult?"

To be able to answer that question, you need to recognize how important parental influence is and the limitations it has. But the short answer is yes, how you raise your child may have a crucial impact on their personality and their mental health later on in life. So, how important is parental influence, and what limitations do you face in how far that influence extends in your child's life?

It's your responsibility, as a parent, to try your best to raise your child in an environment that is warm and loving, with a reasonable amount of discipline and guidance. Parents who give warmth and love to their children, but also set solid limits on their behavior that are upheld with consistency, are offering their children a vital advantage. You are offering your child the opportunity to grow up in an environment that is psychologically healthy for them.

However, as a parent, it is important to understand that there are limitations to what and how much you can do for your child. There are a variety of factors that play a role in determining how your child turns out as an adult.

- A person's athletic ability.
- How physically attractive they are.
- Their intellectual abilities.
- Their temperament.
- How resilient they are.
- Peer pressure and how they relate to those peers.

Both parents and a child's peers may exert an equal amount of influence over a child's development but peers may have the upper hand over the parents. Peer pressure is a huge influence on any child.

As a parent, you need to realize that while raising your child, mistakes will be made. No parent is perfect, for we are all human; however, those mistakes that parents make won't have a large impact on your child when you raise them in a home environment that is filled with concern for their well-being and love. Realizing that their parents are, in fact, imperfect does no harm to children. Coming to terms with the fact that their parents are only human may actually help children accept that they, themselves, are imperfect and only human.

In most cases, when a child is raised by responsible and caring parents who do their best to do right by their child, a good upbringing will have a positive influence and result in a well-adjusted adult. However, you must realize that you can't demand or guarantee success from your child. Every child will eventually determine their own course, and there are times when that course is more heavily influenced by external factors. When children grow up and become adults, they have sole control over their lives and their actions. They will have to bear the brunt of the consequences of those actions. They are responsible for their behavior as adults and must take accountability for it.

When your child grows up, it is important for you to realize and come to terms with the fact that you have tried your best to be a good parent. That means that you have fulfilled your responsibility to your child. You need to realize what you can't control, and not internalize or blame yourself for what wasn't within your control. After everything is said and done, you have tried your best, and it's then up to your child to do the rest.

Temperament and Influence

A child's temperament is not something that either you or they have control over. Temperament is defined as those personality traits of an individual that are based on their biology. In the previous chapter, we discussed the different aspects that make up your temperaments, such as your sociability and energy levels. Temperament is something that you are born with, and the traits you exhibit will remain relatively stable throughout your life. As an example, look at introverted people versus extroverted people. You're not going to truly turn an introverted child into an extrovert. Likewise, you're not going to be able to turn an extroverted child into an introvert.

Temperament plays a big role in how your child will turn out as an adult. One of the reasons for this is how susceptible their personality makes them to external influences such as peer pressure. Children who are more confident, outgoing, have better self-esteem, and who have a more self-assured and dominant personality are less likely to give in to peer pressure. A child who is a people-pleaser and more submissive may fall victim to peer pressure more easily.

You cannot change your child's temperament. You can nurture certain aspects of how they see themselves which may help them to stand more firmly by their beliefs and the family values you instill in them.

Examples of good qualities to nurture in your child:

- Self-esteem
- Confidence
- Self-assurance
- A sense of who they are and where they fit into the world

Nurturing a positive attitude towards themselves may affect how your child perceives external influences; if they feel positively about themselves, they may be more resistant to peer pressure, as opposed to a child who has a negative attitude about themselves.

Peer Pressure

Peer pressure plays a big role in your child's development. They want to fit it and be accepted by others and the friends they make. Peer pressure can put your child under a lot of strain to rebel against your rules, authority, and values. These days, peer pressure presents itself in many forms. For instance, girls are pressured to be attractive and boys are pressured to be buff. Children are influenced by these ideals and values not only directly through media, but also down through the ideals held by peers. Peer pressure makes a child more susceptible to behavior the media puts out, but it may not be in line with your rules or family values. If their peers covet being skinny or having being incredibly muscular, your child may develop a desire for the same. As a parent, you cannot control peer pressure because you cannot control who your child is exposed to. Nurturing the above-listed traits in your child may help them resist peer pressure; however, it's not a foolproof plan.

Environmental Influences

The environment outside of the home to which your child is exposed can be another large contributing factor to their behavior and development. If the neighborhood your child grows up in has an impactful negative element, such as gangs, that negative impact could end up influencing your child. Another example is if your family is culturally different from the surrounding neighborhood, your child could change their behavior to be more culturally in line with those around them. They may even want to shirk their cultural identity in favor of fitting in. Further still, environmental influences come in the form of the media. It's everywhere; you cannot turn in any direction and not be bombarded by the media and the messages being sent to society. Just as temperament may affect susceptibility to peer pressure, the impact of influence from the surrounding environment is further increased or decreased by your child's temperament and peer pressure. Again, nurturing the qualities listed above in your child may help curb the impact that their environment has on influencing them.

The Good News

Your parental influence over your child may be limited, but it is well-known that strong-willed children tend to be confident and self-assured. They stick to their guns, question their influences, and aren't easily swayed by others. This can be seen in their ability to debate until the cows come home, even if their point isn't necessarily right. Raising a strong-willed child in the right environment from a young age, coupled with their exuberant temperament, may go a long way to curbing external influences.

Building a trusting relationship with your child (detailed further in Chapter 7) based upon courteous and open communication between you and your child may also help decrease the impact of external influences. When you have your child's trust and an open line of communication, they will know that they can come to you about any issues they are facing. You will also have the confidence to sit down with them and discuss any issues you may be observing without them feeling judged or ashamed. Good communication and trust are vital aspects of the parent-child relationship and parental influence.

Chapter 4:

Age-Appropriate Behavior

As your child enters toddlerhood, they acquire more freedoms they haven't had before. They learn to walk and explore their world; their independence increases, and new skills are learned. There are various milestones that your pediatrician will use as a gauge to tell whether your toddler is developing at the expected rate. The age range for these milestones varies greatly from child to child; one child may develop faster than others, but this is still considered normal. For instance, prematurely born babies will develop at a slower rate than those carried to full term.

1 Year

At roughly 12 months old your baby transitions to toddler status. In the next few months, your child will learn to walk, use basic words, and start trying to feed themselves. Here's what you can expect at around 12 months (Meduri, 2020):

Language skills and Communication

- Your child will begin referring to you in their first parent-oriented names (e.g. mommy and daddy or mamma and dada) and a couple of other words.
- They will learn about how and when to wave goodbye.
- Your child will start to point at things.

- Babbling and mimicking normal speech using inflection will start.

Physical Development and Movement

- They begin to bang items together using both of their hands.
- They will learn to stand without help.
- Your child may begin walking, eventually with little to no assistance.
- As hand-eye coordination develops, they will start being able to put items into containers and take them out again.
- As messy as it may get, your child may start using their hands to feed themselves.
- They will begin to pick things up using their thumbs and forefingers.

Emotions and Social Development

- They may begin showing pride in learning new skills
- They start taking enjoyment in playing social games, like hide and seek
- They learn to enjoy looking at picture books and listening to stories.
- Separation anxiety may occur, leading to crying when a parent leaves the room.

Learning and Thinking

- As mentioned before, they begin to find enjoyment in looking at books, satiating their curiosity and learning, and will even learn to turn pages on their own.
- Mimicking others' speech and behaviors starts to take place.

- Following single-step commands are starting to happen (e.g. "Pick it up").
- Even though you may not find it entertaining, your child will start performing repetitive behaviors to achieve the desired outcome (e.g. dropping items and picking them up), and this is a vital part of developing curiosity and understanding of their world.

When to Be Concerned

- If they appear to walk with an uneven stride or a limp, or show a distinct weakness on one side of their body.
- Consistently falling forward instead of backward.
- They cannot pick up small items, and don't start using their hands to feed themselves.
- They don't begin pointing at things.
- They aren't babbling and using repeated sounds.
- If they have lost skills they previously learned or have difficulty performing them now.

2 Years

Your toddler has entered what is known as the 'terrible twos.' Why is it called the 'terrible twos'? At this age, their young brains simply have not physically developed enough to handle the surge of impulses and emotions they are feeling. This is when acting out starts to kick in, and your job as a parent gets a little tougher. Keep in mind that this is all natural behavior. So, what can you expect at around 24 months of age? ("2-3 years," n.d.)

Language Skills

- Girls often start talking before boys. They will begin naming family members, objects, body parts, etc. They will be able to point at items when they are named.
- They start being able to follow simple instructions.
- They are able to speak simple sentences of two to four words.
- They begin repeating words they hear.

Movement and Motor Skills

- Being able to stand on tiptoe.
- Staggering while walking will reduce, and then stop altogether.
- Able to throw a ball using an overhand throw.
- They will be able to walk up and down stairs while holding onto the railings.
- Possibly to your chagrin, they start climbing onto and off of furniture unassisted.
- They can carry several smaller toys or one large toy while walking.
- Can kick a ball.

Hand and Finger Development

- They will begin scribbling.
- Building towers using four or more blocks.
- Turning a container over to empty the contents. (Provide them with their own containers of appropriate contents to do this with. It will save you a lot of cleaning up to.)
- Coordinated wrist, palm, and finger movements get a lot better.

Emotional and Social Skills

- Mimicking others continues and improves.

- They will start to display visible excitement when they are around other children.
- Even though they may show excitement around other children, they may play on their own, or next to others but not with them.
- Increasing independence.
- Increasing defiance.
- Developing self-awareness.
- Mood swings, tantrums, and refusals.

Learning and Thinking Skills

- They will start being able to find things even when those things are hidden from view under layers of other stuff.
- Sorting colors and shapes will develop.
- Their use of sentence structure and vocabulary is improving.
- Your child will be able to engage in simple make-believe.
- They can now follow two-part instructions.

Screen Time

- They will enjoy, and possibly ask for, screen time.
  - Screen time is defined as time spent in front of any kind of screen, including mobile phones, TVs, laptops or computers, tablets, etc.
  - No more than 60 minutes per day.
  - No unsupervised screen time.
  - Too much screen time, even for older children, can impede development; however, we are living in a technologically driven age and will have to allow them a little bit of screen time.

When to Be Concerned

- If your child is unable to walk properly after several months of practice.
- They cannot say two-worded sentences.
- If your child does not mimic the words or actions of those around them.
- Can't follow simple instructions.
- Withdrawn/doesn't seek attention.
- If your child doesn't make eye contact with you or anyone else.
- If your child is violent (especially being argumentative, aggressive, or physically violent toward themselves or others).

Help Toddler Development

- Read to them and tell them stories.Encourage them to practice and develop daily skills (e.g. using a spoon).
- Provide opportunities for your child to enjoy some social play.
- Engage in simple conversations with your child to help develop vocabulary and language skills.

Tantrums: What's Not Normal

- Self-injury during the tantrum.
- If tantrums consistently involve physical violence (more than 50% of the time).
- Frequency of their outbursts (10 to 20 per day).
- If your child displays an inability to calm themselves.
- Long outbursts (25 minutes or longer).

Tips for Surviving the Terrible Twos

- Praise good behavior, ignore misbehavior.

- Maintain regular sleep and meal schedules.
- Avoid yelling at your child.
- Maintain your calm.
- Distract and redirect undesirable behavior.
- Make simple rules with short and easy explanations that your child can understand.
- Don't spank your child.
- Offer choices between two things to satisfy their growing independence.
- Don't cave to their demands.
- Maintain a safe home environment.

3 - 4 Years

Your little one is growing up fast and developing at what seems like a phenomenal rate! Time seems to fly by as they master developmental milestones and progress further with movement, thinking, and language skills. Let's take a look at what you can expect to be happening during the age of three to four years (Stewart, 2016; Marks, 2010):

Language Skills

- They can understand basic language rules.
- Your child's vocabulary should be around 500 plus words.
- Intelligible speaking 80% of the time.
- They should be able to say their name.
- They should have the ability to answer the question "How old are you?"
- Sentences should consist of six or more words.
- Mimicking speech sounds is improving.
- Your child will begin using plurals and pronouns.

- You will observe frustration when they are being misunderstood due to mispronunciation of their words.

Motor Skills

- They lose their baby fat between the ages of three and four years.
- An increase in muscle control is evident.
- They will be growing in height.
- An increase in agility is evident.
- He or she will develop the ability to catch a ball with both of their arms extended from their body.
- They can jump down from an 18-inch height using both feet to take off and land.
- An increased interest in tool-like objects (e.g. scissors) will develop.
- Your child will begin using alternative feet to walk up and down staircases.
- They develop the ability to bend over forwards without falling down face-first.
- The ability to draw circles is developing or has already developed quite well.
- Your child will be able to cut a piece of paper into two pieces. (They aren't necessarily cut in straight lines or equal pieces.)
- Increasing concentration while learning precise hand/finger movements.

Emotional and Social Skills

- Decreasing selfishness and an increased ability to share with others.
- Increasing independence.
- The ability to develop friendships will increase.

- The ability to display a wide variety of emotions is developing.
- Your child will develop an awareness of others and their feelings.
- They will start identifying gender and traditionally gender-based activities. (Boys and girls will be able to identify that they are different and start separating in their preferred play activities.)
- An increased interest in structured games will develop.
- They will start developing a sense of time (e.g. They will be able to begin telling the difference between day and night.)
- Your child's imaginative play will grow and increase.
- They will develop a sense of spatial awareness where they become conscious of where their body is in proximity to objects and other people around them.
- At this age, your child will develop a feistier attitude and increased resistance. (At this point in their development the word 'no' becomes somewhat of a favorite.)
- There will be an increase in their desire to please you and others.
- He or she will be able to grasp the concept of ownership and what is theirs and what belongs to others.

When to be Concerned

- If your child is unable to throw a ball using an overhand throw.
- If they are unable to jump on the spot with both feet.
- If they are not able to ride a tricycle.
- If they display a visible difficulty using stairs.
- Frequent falling.
- If they cannot hold crayons between their thumb and forefinger.
- If they are having difficulties scribbling or copying a circle.
- An inability to construct sentences of more than three words.
- Unable to appropriately use "me" or "you" when referring to themselves and others.

- If they are having difficulty speaking.
- If they are unable to build a tower of four blocks and have difficulty handling small items.
- Extreme separation anxiety.
- Lacking responsiveness to their friends or family members.
- If there isn't an increase in their self-control.
- If they have an inability to understand easy commands.

Survival Tips

- Name behaviors and emotions (kindness, patience, etc.).
- Positive parenting: Less yelling and more loving.
- Consistency is all-important.
- Tune into them by putting yourself in their shoes and meeting needs accordingly.
- Use creativity to redirect misbehavior.
- Give them positive contact (e.g. hugs) frequently during the day and say, "I love you."
- Care for yourself.
- Offer small doses of attention frequently.
- Predict repeat offenses before they happen so that you can avoid them.
- Make your expectations clear.
- Know and understand what their other caregivers are doing (e.g. nursery school).
- Teach them compliance.
- Praise their effort, not the outcome of the effort.
- Use a behavior chart with stickers to show them when they behave and then misbehave.
- Resort to time-outs only when all other methods fail.

4 - 5 Years

Your child is now really growing up and is no longer considered a toddler. They are a 'big boy/girl' now, and their independence is ever increasing. They have opinions and thoughts of their own, their confidence is growing, and they may even be developing some sense of self-control. At this stage of their development, children are learning to better express themselves and their needs. Here's what you can expect of four and five year olds (Alli, 2018):

Language and Cognitive Skills

- Developing better conversational skills.
- Your child's vocabulary will increase.
- Thought processes are getting better.
- They are able to answer simple questions more logically.
- Better self-expression.
- They enjoy rhyming, singing, and making up their own words.
- This is the silly and energetic phase, but can also be obnoxious and rowdy.
- Use of increasingly complex sentences.
- They are able to count 10 (or more) items.
- Able to accurately name three shapes and four colors (or more).
- They will begin recognizing some alphabetical letters. (They may even be able to write their own name, but it's not worrisome if they can't.)
- They have a better understanding of time and routine.
- Increased attention span.
- Your child is now able to follow two or three-part commands.
- Recognition of familiar words and instructions (e.g. "Stop") increases.
- They should be able to remember their own address and telephone number.

Movement and Motor Skills

- Running.
- Hopping.
- Kicking and throwing balls.
- Swinging.
- Standing on one foot for at least nine seconds.
- Walking up and down stairs unassisted.
- Walking forward and backward with ease.
- They should be able to pedal a tricycle unassisted.
- They can copy various basic shapes.
- They can now draw a human with a body and several body parts such as arms and legs.
- They should be able to stack at least 10 blocks (or more).
- Your child is using a spoon and a fork.
- Needing little to no assistance completing basic needs tasks (dressing and undressing, brushing teeth, etc.).

Social and Emotional Skills

- Self-centeredness decreases.
- The ability to resolve conflicts increases.
- Increased emotional control.
- They enjoy playing with others.
- They enjoy pleasing their friends.
- They can now understand the rules of games.
- The ability to share and take turns increases.
- They have a better understanding of the rules and compliance with those rules.
- Independence increases.
- Their ability to verbally express their emotions, such as anger, increases without them resorting to physical violence as a form of expression.

When to be Concerned

- If your child displays intense fear, aggression, or shyness.
- If they experience intense separation anxiety.
- If they are unable to focus on a single task for more than five minutes at a time.
- If your child is antisocial.
- If they have only a limited number of interests.
- An inability to recite his or her full name.
- Low levels of imaginative play.
- Constant sadness or unhappiness
- Your child has an inability to display a wide variety of emotions.
- If they have an inability to stack more than eight blocks.
- If your child is experiencing difficulties holding crayons.
- Difficulties sleeping, toileting, or eating.
- Difficulties with daily tasks without assistance (washing hands, brushing teeth, dressing, and undressing, etc.).
- If they lose previously learned skills or now have difficulty performing them.

6 Years Old

Your child is ever-growing and the huge milestone of beginning school is imminent, or they may already have started school. This is one of those super proud-parent moments, and you're sure to take lots of photos. Your child's development is still at a critical stage where they are learning a substantial amount from environmental and external influences. Let's take a look at what you can expect from your six-year-old (Davis, 2017):

Education and Language

- They are now using simple, but full sentences of five to seven words (or more).

- They have the ability to follow three commands consecutively.
- Your child will begin to understand that some words have multiple meanings.
- They will begin to understand simple puns and jokes.
- Your child is beginning to express their sense of humor verbally.
- There is increased growth of cognitive ability.
- They will begin to read age-appropriate books.
- Sounding out new words they are not familiar with.
- The ability to focus on an activity for 15 minutes (or more) will develop.
- They begin to understand numbers instead of just being able to count them.
- Your child should be able to differentiate between left and right, and day and night with ease.
- They are now able to tell time, even if their perception of time passing isn't quite as developed as yours.
- They can now say three numbers backward.

Keep an eye out for cognitive developmental delays

- If they are experiencing reading difficulties.
- If they are showing signs of a possible disability.
- If they seem like they are being bothered by something (e.g. bullying).
- If they seem stressed.
- If they are displaying possible mental health problems.

Overall Development

- Baby teeth begin to be replaced by adult teeth.
- There should be an average growth of four to seven pounds and 2 ½ inches per year now.

- They will begin to develop a sense of body image.
- There will be possible complaints about leg aches and tummy aches as they become more aware of their bodies (make sure there is no real injury or illness).
- Your child is still learning about distance, sound, and speed and must still be kept away from the road for their safety.

Emotional and Social Skills

- Increasing independence from their parents.
- There is an increase in peer pressure and their desire for peer acceptance.
- There is a greater gender association and a separation of the genders during play.
- They will begin or are making their own decisions about toys and sports. Ensure that a wide range is available for them to be exposed to.
- They are beginning to develop a broader attention span.
- Their ability to understand teamwork is increasing, and so is their ability to play organized sport.
- Increasing verbal skills allow better self-expression.
- Lying and cheating may be expected.

How to Help Development

- Limit screen time.
- Read to your child, and have them read to you.
- Use parental control on technology (e.g. TV, smartphones, and computers).
- Encourage self-expression and support the development of self-esteem.
- Discuss topics that may impact your child (E.g. Peer pressure, bullying).

- Teach fire safety and swimming lessons for safety around pools, etc.

Chapter 5:

You're a figure of Authority

One of the biggest obstacles parents of strong-willed children face, and arguably one of the hardest, is being able to assert yourself as an authority while maintaining positive and loving parenting. These children are super spirited and, at times, they can feel like they are too much to handle. You may feel more and more frustrated the more your child acts out. You may feel powerless to control your child's behavior and mold them into a healthy, balanced adult in the making. A pitfall to avoid is starting to resent your child or withdraw as a figure of parental authority, caving in to your child's demands, and losing control. Let's look at effective strategies to gain, and maintain, your position as an authority figure in your child's life.

What Is Parental Authority?

Parental authority denotes your responsibilities and rights over your child from the moment they are born until they turn 18. Simply put, it is your position of authority over your child. When you appear to be a true authoritative figure, you inspire your child to comply with requests and rules and to emulate your behavior. Your children will look up to you as a role model instead of trying to exert themselves as the ones in charge. Asserting your parental authority better allows you to take control so that you ensure your child's healthy development and safety through providing structure.

Why Is Structure Important?

Structure is incredibly important in a child's life. As a parent, you are setting limits and boundaries that affect almost every aspect of your child's life. When a clear structure is imposed, children learn to predict how others will react. They also learn how to behave properly, and it teaches them what kinds of behavior are unacceptable. A good structure offers them a sense of their place in the world. They learn about right, wrong, and the consequences of their actions. There are several specific reasons structure is important.

Safety

Structure offers children limitations that protect, not only their physical safety, but also their emotional security.

The World and People

Within safe boundaries, children are taught about the world and people around them, and how to properly behave and treat them.

Handling Frustration and Disappointment

These two emotions are a natural part of life, and children without structure may not learn to handle them appropriately in a constructive manner. Structure teaches children to appreciate delayed gratification as opposed to instant gratification, an important life skill for the future.

Developing Responsibility

Limitations on their behavior teach children self-control and how to make responsible decisions.

Providing Structure

There are several ways in which parents provide structure for their children. Let's delve into how you provide structure for your strong-willed child.

Structure in Their Environment

This often refers to controlling the activities your child participates in and how they spend their time. You will be required to supervise and monitor your child by being mentally and physically available to them. If someone else is in charge, such as at a daycare, you will have to make sure that they are competent to do so in your stead.

Daily Routines

Routines are an important part of structuring your child's life in order to provide them with a sense of predictability and security. When a child doesn't feel secure in their environment and their place in the world, it can lead to confusion that results in acting out. This is especially true of strong-willed children who are exuberant and can lead to power struggles.

Effective Discipline

Managing your child's behavior through effective discipline strategies that don't harm your child physically, mentally, or emotionally will keep them safe and allow them to develop to their full potential. This is done in two ways. First, you teach your child good behavior, such as cleaning their room. The second way is that you set boundaries against unacceptable behavior.

Parental Flexibility

- Children change as they grow. Parents may need to adjust parenting strategies to suit the child's needs.
- Overly rigid parenting may result in complications such as smothering self-identity.
- Flexible parenting can help to negotiate difficult situations better.
- Children and parents may negotiate rules and consequences and adjust them without parents giving up their parental authority by caving to demands.

Independence

While providing structure for your child is important, you should allow your child to slowly gain independence. When it is both appropriate and safe, allowing a child to make their own decision may be beneficial. Allow them to make their own choices and experience natural consequences. Natural consequences often lead to learning and, when appropriate, may be more effective than instituting limits and consequences.

Allowing children to make their own decisions and learn from them sends the message that you trust them to make the right decision and builds their confidence. This develops healthy self-esteem and strengthens your child-parent relationship. Making their own decisions also reaches self-responsibility, reducing dependence.

Don't confuse independence and flexibility with permissiveness or a lack of supervision or attention. Being too rigid or too permissive is equally damaging.

Child-Parent Relationship

The quality and strength of your child-parent relationship will enhance your parental authority and the effectiveness of your positive discipline. The stronger that relationship, the stronger your child's desire to behave in a way that garners approval and aligns itself with your values. The willingness of a parent to cooperate with their child leads to a reciprocating willingness of the child to cooperate with the parent.

The Dangers of Losing Authority

Becoming a permissive parent and losing your parental authority is a pitfall many parents fall victim to. Sure, permissive parenting means you seem like a fun parent, being warm and friendly all the time. However, when does being friendly become too friendly for your child's wellbeing?

Permissive parents find themselves unable to refuse their children anything and avoid enforcing discipline in case they lose their status as their child's BFF. This can be a slippery slope that you don't want to find yourself sliding down.

What Is a Permissive Parent?

- It is one of the three main parenting types.
- Permissive parenting is distinguished by inconsistency, as well as lacking a structure and limits for discipline.

Rules and respect go hand in hand. Permissive parenting lacks rules, which lead to children not having respect for themselves or those around them. This can have a detrimental effect on their interactions with their peers and figure of authority, such as teachers.

Traits of Permissive Parents

- They provide little to no rules.

- They are inconsistent in enforcing the rules.
- Permissive parents prefer parent-child friendship over parental authority.
- They take their child's opinion into account for big decisions and allow this input to sway their decision.
- They place an emphasis on freedom instead of responsibility.
- They prefer to have the natural consequences of their child's decisions to take place instead of imposing rules and consequences.
- They are not too concerned about safety and view dangerous situations as opportunities for learning.

Positives of Permissiveness

When some permissiveness is employed with thoughtful execution on the right child, it can have its benefits.

- A child's self-assurance is built from self-expression and a willingness to try new things despite possible consequences.
- Creativity is encouraged through children experimenting with a wide range of experiences.
- Children are afforded more freedom to explore their world and discover new things.

Negatives of Permissiveness

Permissiveness has its positives, but also its negatives. Here's how permissive parenting can negatively affect your child. (This is especially true for strong-willed children, as they are natural risk-takers with a strong will to override their parents wherever possible.)

- Children don't learn right from wrong without a clear set of boundaries.
- Children lacking boundaries are prone to risk-taking behavior without fear of consequences. As natural risk-takers, strong-

willed children may easily take part in risky behaviors like substance abuse.

- Permissive parents may give the impression that their child should keep their problems to themselves which can lead to withdrawing, depression, and anxiety.
- Permissive parenting lets children be their own bosses, which encourages a rebellious attitude within and outside of the home.
- You aren't providing them with a role model.
- Permissive parenting can break down your self-respect as a parent due to allowing your strong-willed child too much free-rein to be unruly.
- Children become self-centered without a healthy respect for others. (Perry, 2019)

Permissive Parenting Examples

- You allow them unlimited screen time.
- You offer them unlimited access to food and treats which may lead to malnutrition and childhood obesity.
- Children are allowed to play despite not having followed any rules to earn the privilege.

Permissive parenting isn't always a healthy parenting style for children, especially exuberant children. They do not learn to curb their behaviors and don't learn important life skills. By trying to constantly win your child's approval, you risk endangering them. You aren't their best friend; you are their parent, and it's your job to enforce the rules to keep them safe and healthy.

Now we have established that permissive parenting isn't a good option when raising a strong-willed child; however, the opposite isn't necessarily healthy either. Being an authoritarian parent may be just as detrimental to the development of a healthy, well-adjusted adult.

The Dangers of Abusing Parental Authority

The characteristics of authoritarian parenting are an emphasis on strictness and sternness, and an insistence on obedience without question. Good behavior is enforced through rewards for good behavior and misbehavior results in punishments, such as shaming. These parents are also prone to be less responsive and cold towards their children. This can cause a child to develop various developmental problems.

Behavioral Problems

- Authoritarian parenting doesn't bring about long-term improvement in the behavior of children.
- Extreme control often causes an increase in misbehavior over time.
- Being too strict and controlling often leads to an increased risk of exhibiting behavior that is defiant, aggressive, anti-social, and disruptive.
- Children of authoritarian parents are more prone to engaging in substance abuse.

Resourcefulness and Social Skills

- Children are less resourceful and suffer social skills development issues.
- They are more likely to get involved in bullying, both as the victim and the bully.

Emotional Problems

- Children of authoritarian parents are at higher risk of developing depression, low self-esteem, and anxiety.

- They have more difficulty with emotional regulation.
- Children may develop depersonalization which makes them feel disconnected from themself.

Education

- Children who are shamed for performing poorly tend to perform even more poorly in problem-solving
- Children of authoritarian parents tend to achieve more poorly academically.

Morality

- Children are prone to poor self-regulation capabilities and lack adequate moral reasoning abilities.
- They are prone to tuning their parents out as they mature.

Authoritarian parenting may be detrimental to strong-willed children, especially as it brings about power struggles when the child and parent clash. This may cause the parent to become even harsher and stricter. If this happens, the child may grow to resent their parents and learn how to misbehave behind the scenes without getting caught. Their strong will being in opposition to their parents can create a stressful home environment, and may lead to psychiatric problems, even as adults.

Parents should aim for the middle of the road approach to parenting without being too lenient or too strict. This way, children learn a healthy respect for boundaries while still being able to grow into their full potential.

Parenting Style: Finding the Balance

There are four main types of parenting:

- Authoritative
- Permissive
- Uninvolved
- Authoritative (Bright, 2020)

While authoritative may seem very similar to authoritarian, they are completely different. Authoritative parenting is that sweet spot right in the middle between too strict and too lenient. This is what you should be aiming for as your parenting style when dealing with a strong-willed child.

Characteristics of Authoritative Parenting

- These parents are level-headed and caring.
- They set high (but not unreasonable) and precise expectations for their children.
- They are self-disciplined.
- Authoritative parents explain the reasons behind the rules they set and these rules are clearly defined.
- They communicate frequently with their child in an age-appropriate manner.

Positive Authority

Being a positive authority in your child's life means:

- Your kindness shows that you love your child and respect their personal limitations and their individual needs.

- Your firmness offers your child structure, ensures their safety, and offers a healthy environment in which they can develop and learn.

Becoming an Authoritative Parent

- Validate their emotions through acknowledgment and recognize how emotions affect behavior. Correct their behavior, not their emotions, and teach them
- Allow your child to make small, age-appropriate decisions for themselves.
- Listen to your child's opinions, ideas, and concerns. Positive attention helps to prevent many behavioral problems.
- appropriate coping and self-expression methods.
- Set up clear rules, state expectations precisely, and explain the reasoning behind those rules.
- Provide incentive motivation to promote good behavior.
- Consider their feelings when making decisions that affect them, but don't let them overrule your decisions.
- Give your child a single warning for small transgressions.
- Set consequences for their misbehavior to teach them life lessons appropriate to the transgression.
- Teach them to learn from their mistakes by helping them to find appropriate solutions.
- Strike a balance between responsibility and freedom by allowing them the freedom to perform tasks independently, as long as they follow the rules.
- Teach your child self-discipline to nurture the development of their self-control.
- Nurture a healthy parent-child relationship.

Regaining Authority After It's Lost

If you are a parent who has lost their parental authority, don't despair. You can regain that authority. You must start embracing and employing your authority through positive authoritative parenting. Teach your child that they live by your rules as long as they are living under your roof. You don't have to be an authoritarian. When you employ positive parenting, your child will feel valued instead of oppressed. Be a role model that they look up to, and remember your child is always watching you. They will learn more from your behavior than you could imagine, so you need to behave as if you are always being watched.

Communicating Authority

Strong-willed children develop better under parental authority instead of being left to their own devices. These children are often exuberant and don't stop to think about the possible consequences of their actions. This lack of taking a moment to consider those consequences may result in them putting themselves in situations that threaten their safety.

Embrace Your Parental Role

- Employ positive authority.
- Provide your child with a clear structure.
- Be clear about your family values.
- Set rules that are in accordance with your family values.
- Discuss rules with your child so that they clearly understand what is expected of them and the consequences of breaking those rules.

Consistency

- Stick to your family rules, don't allow any amount of complaining to sway you from caving to your child's whims.
- Clearly communicate what your expectations are by using age-appropriate language.
- Set clear limits on what behavior is acceptable and what is not.
- Consistently enforce your family rules with consequences that are age-appropriate and suitable for the misbehavior.

Expect Challenges

- Challenges to your authority are a normal part of childhood for any child, but even more so with a strong-willed child. Expect them to push back against your parental authority often.
- Remain calm in the face of misbehavior and challenges to your authority.
- Maintain control over every situation. It's not enough to have self-control; you need to remain in control of the situation to avoid your child questioning your authority even further.
- Be consistent with consequences; don't let misbehavior go unchecked at any time, not even once.
- Offer your child opportunities to follow the rules such as making small decisions themselves.
- The discipline employed should fit the behavior and the individual child. This way you can use the discipline to teach them life lessons. Using discipline that doesn't suit your child's temperament and personality won't be as effective and may lead to further misbehavior.
- Anticipate challenges and know the consequences. Being unsure of consequences makes you appear to be wavering which will lead to your child questioning your authority further.

Chapter 6:

Constructive Communication

Courtesy is an integral part of raising a strong-willed child and cementing that parent-child relationship. Courtesy is in decline in our modern society, and that is, unfortunately, includes parent-child courtesy as well. Your child is exposed to various external instances of courtesy, and it is important to set a good example through your own dealings with them.

What Is Courteous Communication?

There are seven Cs for courteous communication (Mulder, 2013):

- Clear: Don't leave room for assumption; make your message very clear. Leaving room for error is setting your child up for transgressions.
- Correct: Use age-appropriate words and words that cannot be misconstrued as having more than one meaning.
- Complete: When communicating with your child, provide them with all the information they need to know.
- Concise: Don't give long-winded explanations or lectures. Be as concise as possible, especially with younger children who cannot process large amounts of information in one go.
- Concrete: Believe in what you are saying. Your conviction will impress the seriousness of the discussion on your child.
- Coherent: The discussion must have a logical flow; don't go back and forth or change from one subject to another. Stick to

one subject and don't refer to past behavior, as your child is more focused on the present.

- Courteous: Check your tone and word usage. When explaining rules and consequences use 'I' statements. Instead of placing the blame on your child, state how their behavior makes you feel. (E.g. "I feel hurt when you talk back to me," instead of, "Your back talking is unacceptable!")

In addition to those, there are several ways in which to instill courtesy in your child

- Parent First: You are your child's first role model. By being courteous to your child, you encourage them to be courteous to you and others in return.
- Tolerance: Teach your child about the differences in others' beliefs, abilities, and backgrounds, and to be tolerant of others who are different or hold different views.
- Reading People: People have different emotional cues, such as body language and facial expressions. Teach your child how to read at least the most basic and recognizable of these cues, and to adjust their behavior or communication accordingly.
- Manners: Teach your child how having good manners affects their interaction with others, and how others will see them more positively when they have good manners.
- Help: Get involved in some form of service to your local community to teach them how to help others willingly.

Conclusion

Being courteous, but not a pushover, will strengthen communication with your child and encourage their compliance and respect. If you respect them, they are more likely to respect you. If you teach your child courtesy toward you and others, you change the way in which they see and react to the world around them.

How to Be Courteous to Your Child

When you are teaching your child to be courteous to you and others, you should lead by example.

- Be courteous to them, and teach them the seven Cs of courtesy by performing them yourself when you interact with your child and others.
- Instill good manners in them by having good manners yourself.
- Always give them a reason why when setting the rules; part of courtesy is giving others the opportunity to understand.
- Praise them when they have good manners to reinforce that it's a good thing.
- Make developing good manners a game; children love games and learn a lot from interactive play.

The Power of Discourtesy

When you are discourteous to your child, you are setting a precedent and can cause them long-term harm.

Being discourteous to your child can:

- Demonstrate a lack of care on your behalf.
- Cause your emotional and psychological harm to your child by negatively impacting their self-esteem, undermining their value, damaging their confidence, and reducing their ability to take initiative.
- It can impact how they treat you and others. Why should they be courteous if you aren't courteous to them? Being discourteous to your child also instills in them that discourtesy is normal and acceptable behavior.

Beware

- Don't foster contempt by enforcing rules that are too harsh or giving them the "Because I said so" answer to their questions.
- Don't use deconstructive criticism or blame; constructive feedback in the discussion is more effective.
- Don't take their cooperation for granted. Learn to appreciate each time they cooperate.
- Don't neglect physical affection; children thrive when they are reminded of your love for them, and physical affection is a very effective expression of your love for them.
- Never ignore your child.
- Don't exclude your child in discussions or in activities they show interest in.

Employing Praise Correctly

Praise is a vital part of a child's healthy development, but parents need to know how to use it to their advantage wisely.

Children need praise not only when accomplishing something noteworthy. Appreciating and praising some of the small things can go a long way to encouraging cooperation. However, make the level of praise appropriate to the behavior.

- Don't go overboard with your praise. You will teach your child that even the tiniest things warrant praise. When they don't get it in the 'real world,' such as at school, they will act out in response to the lack of praise.
- When achievements come easily to your child, avoid too much praise. Praise is good but a simple hug and, "Well done," will suffice.

- Avoid insincere praise, children pick up on your sincerity and may develop insecurities or a nonchalant attitude toward rules in response to your insincerity.
- Offer praise for behavior your child can control more than accomplishments they show a gifted ability for.
- Beware of showering your child with praise for things they enjoy doing; it may encourage them to neglect the things they aren't good at.
- Don't compare your child to others and only praise them when they out-do the others. Acknowledge your child's individual abilities.

When to Apologize

Many people feel uncomfortable owning up to their mistakes and apologizing for them. As adults, we are quick to insist that children apologize to others for a transgression, but what about when we make mistakes? Parents are human too, and we make mistakes. We aren't always right, no matter how much we would like to believe that. Apologizing to our children when we mess up is a vital part of maintaining a healthy parent-child relationship. Just because you're apologizing doesn't mean that your child will have less respect for you. They will still know who's in charge and won't see an apology as a chance to undermine your authority. Instead, you are earning their respect because you can get down on their level and apologize when you need to.

The Power of Apology

What wrong things are we teaching our children when we refuse to apologize to them or to others?

- Apologizing takes on an element of shame.
- Apologizing equates to bad behavior or actually being bad.
- When you damage a relationship and don't apologize, that's okay.
- An apology is something that only gets done when you are pressured to do it.
- You lose your status when you apologize.

When you model the behavior of apologizing to others, you are teaching your child valuable lessons.

- Everybody makes mistakes; everyone needs to own up to them, and make amends.
- Everybody sometimes hurts those around them. It's important for us to acknowledge that we've hurt someone and make amends.
- Offering an apology often makes the other person feel better about you.
- Apologizing isn't shameful and it can make us feel better.
- You are teaching them the difference between wrong and right.
- You are setting a good example so they won't repeat the 'wrong' behavior.
- Apologizing to your child when you have done wrong, and they know you've done wrong, can help them become less stubborn.
- You're teaching your child how to communicate their misbehaviors in an appropriate way.

When to Apologize to Your Child

- Consider apologizing for even the little things. If you acted in a way you don't want your child to behave, it's time to apologize.

- Even if you don't think something is a big deal, but your child does, it's worth acknowledging their feelings and offering an apology.
- Your apology must acknowledge how your behavior affected your child and their feelings.
- Don't play the blame game. Don't make excuses by blaming your child or anything else; own your mistake. Making excuses for your behavior teaches your child to do the same.
- Apologizing teaches accountability through taking responsibility. (E.g. If you weren't around to help your child work through a conflict with another person, then apologizing for not being there helps model accountability for neglecting your responsibility.)

Teaching Your Child How to Apologize

Don't Punish

- Have your child offer a verbal apology and an act of kindness to make amends.
- Ask your child what they think they could do to make amends.

Don't Lecture

- Ask your child about what they were feeling when they misbehaved to help them understand their emotions in relation to their actions.
- Teach them to see how their behavior affected the other person by asking how they think their actions made that person feel.

- Teach them to take responsibility by acknowledging the emotions and that even though their feelings were valid, their response was not.

Roleplay

- Offer your child the opportunity to enact a pretend 're-do' and ask them how they could handle the situation better.
- Allow them time to think about alternative responses.
- Practicing with you provides an opportunity to make better decisions next time.

Tip: Allow time between the misbehavior and the apology for your child's emotions to simmer down. They may be more willing and more sincere when offering an apology.

When to Forgive and Move On

As a parent, you have to come to terms that you are not 'super mom/dad.' You are human, and you are going to feel human emotions. There are going to be times your child's actions cause you to feel a variety of negative emotions from frustration and anger to feeling hurt. There are times that these hurtful actions can place strain on the parent-child relationship. You may not be a 'super parent' but you are an adult and it's your job to forgive your child and not hold grudges.

Respect Their Choices

- You can try to help them onto a better path, but they may resist.
- Older children may make decisions that disappoint you (e.g. drugs, recklessness, crime, etc.).

- If you've done your very best to try to help, realize that they have made their own decisions.
- Let them face the natural consequences of their actions.
- Respect their need for individuality from you.

Make an Empathic Connection

- Explain to your child that their actions have hurt you.
- Use age-appropriate language to ensure they understand.
- Have them apologize.
- Don't guilt-trip them, but teach them to empathize with your feelings.

Maintain Open Communication

- Let them know that they can always talk to you and that you will listen.
- Don't lock your child out when they've hurt you.
- Maintaining open communication may help to teach empathy.
- Communication means talking about what affects both of you.
- Return to normalcy
- Maintain routine interactions such as family dinners.
- Make an effort to return to normalcy during the forgiveness process.
- Returning to normalcy isn't denial.
- Returning to normalcy demonstrates your forgiveness and willingness to mend the relationship.

Be Their Parent

- Take a time-out to regain your calm and control.
- You must be the bigger person.

- When your child hurts you, don't use guilt trips, sulk, or give them the silent treatment.
- Teach them empathy by being empathic yourself.
- You must not withhold love and care just because they've hurt you.
- Discuss their actions. They may not be empathic toward you but they need your empathy.

Self-Interests vs. Their Best Interests

It may sometimes be easy to confuse what is in your child's best interest for their own sake, and what is in their best interest for your sake. It's important that you make a distinction between the two so that you always act in a way that best benefits your child.

- Don't judge your parental capabilities by your child's performance.
- Don't allow your insecurities to dictate your self-esteem based on your child's performance.
- Don't give the impression that your reputation as a good parent is dependent on their performance.
- Your child may feel it is their responsibility to make you happy and depend on your approval to validate their own self-worth.
- Don't compare your child to others or your own performance.
- Maintain self-care and self-development to avoid projecting your desires onto your child.
- Avoid making your child feel guilty if they don't perform well.

Talking Back and Constructive Communication

Talking back may make you feel disrespected and inadequate as a parent. This isn't always the case. Sometimes children are testing boundaries. They may be seeking attention. It may be difficult to not respond with anger but there are ways to combat caving to their misbehavior.

- Be a role model by watching how you speak to your child.
- Watch your language and model values.
- Intervene immediately.
- Firmly impress upon them that the behavior is not acceptable and that they will not receive your attention until they speak to you respectfully.
- Engage your child as often as possible in a positive way to build a connection. Take interest in their interests and spend quality time together.
- Show that you aren't just there to punish.
- Show them that they can always count on you.
- Children give hurting a parent's feelings a second thought when they feel connected, loved, and appreciated. Give them your undivided attention for at least 20 minutes daily.
- Calmly react to their behavior.
- Set clear expectations.
- Don't react with the same level of contempt you perceive from them. Reacting with the same level of disrespect reinforces rude behavior.
- Discuss their behavior, what is acceptable, and what is not.

Chapter 7:

Building Trust

Disciplining a spirited child without breaking that spirit is based on trust. When you reclaim your authority, communicate effectively, and employ a positive authoritative parenting style, you are already well on the road to building that kind of trust with your child! Trust and discipline will allow your child to develop more constructive avenues of communication and improve their behavior.

Building Trust: Emotional Intelligence

Building a relationship of trust between you and your child is vital to curbing misbehavior and encouraging good behavior. When your child trusts you, they are less likely to misbehave or act out because of insecurity. Here's how to use emotional intelligence to build that trusting relationship.

Trust Emotions

Young children often struggle with intense emotions and a lack of emotional regulation. As a parent, when your child acts out, it's tempting to quickly get out of the situation by offering treats, bribes, and distractions. However, this does nothing to build your child's trust in themselves or in you.

- Acknowledge your child's emotions by describing what you deserve in age-appropriate language. (E.g. I see that you are angry with your friend.")

- Help label emotions to increase their emotional literacy. (E.g. "Describe to me how you're feeling.")
- Validate their emotions. (E.g. "I understand why you are angry.") When we validate our children's emotions, we allow them to feel accepted in their emotions instead of rejected.
- Teaching a child to trust is based on the foundation of teaching them about their emotions and how to listen to those emotions.

Take Emotional Responsibility

Taking emotional responsibility can be seen in a situation where your child may be struggling. Instead of rushing to their rescue, it's more beneficial to allow them to express that emotion, such as by crying. This way they learn to take responsibility for their emotional responses to situations, but also learn to trust you as their parent for encouragement and support.

- Teach emotional responsibility by modeling taking responsibility for your own emotions in difficult situations.
- Observing our own emotions allows us to understand the choices we make and pick up on productive and non-productive patterns.
- Discuss with your child ways in which they can take responsibility for their emotions and the consequential behavioral patterns. This teaches them to think about the consequences of their actions before acting out.
- Teaching your child emotional responsibility is setting up the framework for building a trusting relationship.

Balance Trust and Expectation

Your child's trust in you is based on your expectations of them. If you offer them a choice of two things, let them make their own decision without fear of disappointing you. This teaches them that you trust them, allowing them to reciprocate by trusting you.

- Even if your child makes a decision that is different from what you had hoped for, recognize it as their decision. To avoid a conflict of expectation, ensure that all the options you provide are acceptable to you.
- Children have not got a fully developed prefrontal cortex, this means that they won't always think about the consequences of their choices or actions. Teach your child age-appropriate consequential thinking (pros and cons, personal consequences vs. those that affect others, short-term vs. long-term), and having empathy for their developing mental abilities. (DuongDirector et al., 2017)
- By setting clear expectations and offering limited choices that are acceptable, when your child makes their own choice of acceptable behavior without your disappointment, they are learning that you trust them.
- When you don't allow your child the opportunity to take emotional responsibility and overcome obstacles on their own by rushing to the rescue, they are not learning to trust themselves. They also get the impression that you don't trust them.

Building Trust: Behavior

Not only can you help build a strong trusting relationship with your child using emotional intelligence. Trust is also built on your behavior toward your child.

- Don't Break Promises: Even though situations change, don't make promises you can't keep. This is especially important with young children as no matter the reason, they probably won't understand. All they can comprehend is that you Listen: Hear your child out in earnest. Don't use selective listening, judgmental statements, or enter a discussion with an agenda or preconceived ideas. Being heard and valued builds trust.

- Model Behavior: If you want your child to trust you, don't behave differently from what you expect of them. As they say, "Practice what you preach."
- Tell the Truth: Be honest with your child, no exceptions for white lies, and they will trust what you say every time and learn to be honest with you. Lie and deceive them, and they will learn to distrust you and do the same.
- made a promise. Break a promise and you break their trust. If a promise must be broken, discuss it in advance and reschedule if possible.
- Consistency: Implement rules, follow through with rewards or consequences, and keep promises; every time you are consistent, you build that trust.
- Don't Threaten: If you say that you are going to enforce a consequence, follow through. It may seem counterintuitive but when a child can trust what you say, even about consequences, they learn to trust you.
- Respect: Showing your child disrespect instills distrust when communicating with you and how you will generally treat them.
- Appreciate Their Honesty: Express appreciation when your child is honest, whether they tell you how they feel or that they misbehaved. You are building trust that they can come to you about anything and you are building their integrity.

Rituals vs. Routines

The daily, monthly, or even annual rituals you have as a family, paired with your daily or even weekly routine helps develop trust with your child. When they feel secure in the predictability of a routine, they trust you to make everything run like clockwork. When you build that emotional connection and sense of belonging through family rituals, your child will trust you more based on that emotional connection.

Both rituals and routines are particular and repeated activities that take place between two or more members of your family.

Routines

- Routines are functional and hold no special meaning.
- They involve crucial communication that allows everyone to function as a unit.
- Rituals often have a set time constraint.
- The steps of a routine are repeated regularly.
- An example of a routine is getting up at the same time in the morning to go to work or school.

Rituals

- Rituals hold a special meaning.
- They involve meaningful communication that includes the expression of emotions.
- Rituals help to establish and maintain an understanding of what it means to be a member of the family.
- Rituals aren't just about the here and now and might be handed down through generations so they go beyond just the present time.
- Examples of family rituals include traditions (e.g. yearly birthday celebrations), celebrations (e.g. graduations), and interactions that follow a pattern (e.g. family dinners).

The most distinguishing element between routines and rituals is the impact a disruption of the activity will have on the family. Disrupted routines cause inconvenience. Disrupted rituals pose a threat to family bonds. Both play important roles in maintaining the structure and the emotional atmosphere of the daily life of a family. While being different they are both interlaced within daily family interactions (e.g. family meals are neither purely routine nor purely ritual; they encompass aspects of both).

The Importance of Rituals and Routines

In young children, rituals may develop between parent and child. These rituals can calm or enhance emotional experiences such as separation from the parent. They also help a child accept certain aspects of their daily routine that may cause them stress. An example of this is the ritual of saying goodbye to a parent when being left at daycare in the morning. A goodbye ritual helps the child accept the aspect of separation when the morning routine is taking place.

Rituals

- Rituals may increase the child-parent relationship satisfaction by developing an emotional connection.
- They affect your child's emotional development interactions with society as a whole, making regular rituals between parent and child a vital part of their healthy development.
- Rituals contribute to positively developing a child's sense of validation, belonging, and security.
- They offer a child a sense of comfort, especially in times of high emotion or distress. For instance, rituals may help a child better overcome the emotions of sadness and concern associated with an illness in the family.
- Family values are strengthened and conveyed to children, helping them develop those same values.

Routines

- Routines offer children structure which in turn offers them a sense of security through predictability.
- They can help reduce behavioral problems, especially in strong-willed children. Your child feels safe and secure and therefore is less likely to be triggered to act out.
- They establish family expectations and rules, helping your child learn and adhere to these rules.
- Routines can foster independence. When a child is accustomed to a routine, they may want to independently perform certain tasks.
- Constructive habits such as brushing teeth or doing homework are established.
- Routines offer a structured framework in which to fit daily rituals, enhancing emotional and relationship satisfaction. This is important to prevent acting out as your child will be more content.
- Routines offer comfort during times of stress or change such as changing schools or moving house.

Chapter 8:

Establishing Family Rules

Rules are put in place for a reason. Children are not able to learn without being subject to having to follow the rules. These rules guide them through their development as they grow up. Without rules, they will never learn self-discipline, self-control, or how to appropriately deal with their emotions and impulses. The first place a child learns about rules is in the home, which makes family rules an integral part of your daily life on your journey to raising a well-adjusted and healthy spirited child.

What Are Family Rules

Family rules are a set of clear and specific rules that are put in place for the members of your family. Each member is expected to follow these rules, Family rules align with the family's values, and by following these rules every person in the family upholds those shared values. When there are children in the home, these rules help instill in them your family's specific values as they grow up. Family rules are not just observed in the home, they are a guideline for how every member should behave at home and in public or social situations. Each family will have rules that contain elements of the parental values, which may have been handed down through their own parents, as well as their culture, religious beliefs, and more. Therefore, while each family may have rules that overlap with other families, your family rules will be as unique to your family as you are unique as a group.

Why Are Family Rules Important?

The first place your child learns about rules is in the home. From a very young age, you begin imposing rules on them, even if it doesn't seem like much of a rule. For instance, teaching a young child who doesn't yet possess language skills that simply crying for attention isn't acceptable, you are imposing a rule. The rule, in that case, is that you don't cry just to get attention.

- These rules are the first form of structure in your child's life and are the foundation upon which their future behavior is built.
- Family rules help the whole family to function as a cohesive unit.
- Rules help to keep every member of the family safe.
- Family rules help the various members to interact smoothly with each other and strengthen the bonds they have with each other.
- They teach children that there is a right way and a wrong way to behave, and the wrong way won't be tolerated.
- Family rules at home teach your child how to behave and interact with others outside of the home.
- There will be other places where your child will have to follow rules, such as at school. Learning to follow rules at home will set them up to be able to follow rules elsewhere.
- Consistently enforced family rules help your child understand the importance of following rules in any situation.

Rules Are for Everyone

We don't set up family rules for only our children to follow. Every single member of the family must follow the rules that are set out, with no exceptions. As an adult, you may feel that you have earned the right to do as you please; however, when even a single member of the family doesn't follow the rules, your child begins to receive mixed messages. There will be confusion and they will begin to question why they have to follow a rule when nobody else has to. Your child may feel singled out and not understand the reason behind the rule if only they have to follow it. This can lead to conflicts and acting out.

Get Everyone on the Same Page

Consistency in upholding family rules is key to successfully getting your child to follow them. This means that everyone involved, parents and other caregivers such as grandparents, are on the same page about your family rules. Here's how you can bring everyone up to speed and ensure that everyone is working together to follow and enforce your family rules. Remember, if your children are old enough to offer their input, listen to them and take their opinions on board. You don't have to give in to their demands but they may have a point of view that is valid to at least consider. Children may even come up with beneficial ideas that you wouldn't have thought of.

- Talk about which rules would be beneficial to your family.
- Parents and caregivers must collectively agree upon which rules to set for the family. (Children may offer input but they don't get to vote on which rules are being set.)
- Rules must be clear, specific, and manageable for children. You are setting them up for failure if you set unrealistic rules.
- Post or put the rules up in your home so that every single family member knows the rules and it can serve as a reminder so that nobody forgets them.
- Speak with other caregivers who mind your child so that everyone who interacts with your child is on the same page.

Avoid confusion by having one set of rules when they are with one caregiver, but a different set when they are with another.

- Request that all caregivers who mind your child be consistent in monitoring your child and enforcing the rules and their consequences.
- Children may need to be reminded of the rules repeatedly.

Setting Family Rules

Before you start setting rules for your family, take into account the children in your home and their age. Younger children will not be able to remember and adhere to a large number of rules. When you are dealing with younger children, focus on setting a maximum of three vital family rules, to begin with. Once your child has learned those rules and is able to consistently follow them, consider bringing in one or two new rules. You can repeat this process of setting a few new rules at a time until your child is old enough to be following all of the family rules.

Here are some tips on how to set family rules.

Identify Family Rules

- Define rules clearly. Explain the rules to young children in age-appropriate language and make sure they understand the rule.
- Make rules realistic and age-appropriate.
- Make them specific, avoid being vague. Vagueness leaves a grey area that can lead to confusion for your child.
- Examples of come common family rules include:
  - Don't kick or hit others. Keep your feet and hands to yourself.
  - Don't interrupt someone while they are speaking, wait for your turn.

- ○ Don't yell in the house. Use your inside voice when inside the home.
- ○ Don't climb on or jump on the furniture. The couch is for sitting and the bed is for lying in.

Explain Family Rules

- It is important to explain family rules clearly to children. Make sure that they understand the rule by asking them to repeat the rule back to you in his or her own words.
- Very young children may not understand all of the words in a rule. When you tell them not to hurt anyone, you may need to explain what that means. If they do hurt someone, you must explain to them that hitting or kicking is, in fact, hurting and reiterate the rule to them.
- Frequently remind small children of the rules. Using rule charts with pictures instead of words is a good way to remind your toddler of the rules.
- When employing rule charts, use one column for the rule and another column for the consequence.

Follow Family Rules

- Family rules are meant for the whole family, so make sure everyone adheres to them.
- Model the rules for your children by following them yourself. You can't expect a child to be respectful to others if you are not.
- Praise a child when they demonstrate good behavior, don't just focus on disciplining their misbehavior.
- Use lots of praise when a young child is learning a new rule. This encourages good behavior to stick.

- When an exception to a rule is made for any reason (e.g. holidays or special circumstances), explain the exception clearly, why it is being made, and how long the exception will last. When the exception period comes to an end, prepare your child by warning them in advance that it is ending. Remind them that it is ending when it ends and then again after it has ended.

Consequences

- Consistency in enforcing family rules is vitally important.
- Make sure that your child understands the rule as well as the consequence of breaking that rule.
- Follow a broken rule with immediate consequence.
- Include consequences on the rules chart so that you are not only reminding your child of the rule, but also the consequence if that rule is broken.
- All family members are subject to consequences for broken family rules; that goes for you as the parent as well. You will create a lot of confusion in children if they receive consequences for breaking the rule but nothing happens when you break it.

Five Types of Essential Family Rules

Each family will have their own set of rules unique to their family structure, culture, religious views, and even their social status. However, there are five types of rules that every family should have.

Safety

Safety rules include not only physical safety, but emotional safety as well. When your strong-willed child follows safety rules, they will be free to expend their energy on learning, exploring, and playing.

An example of a physical safety rule: Don't answer the door without an adult present.

Morality

These rules are set to instill your family's moral values in your child.

An example of a moral rule: Apologizing for wrongdoing.

Healthy Habits

Structure and routine help a child develop and function at their best. Set family rules that will encourage the development of healthy daily habits.

An example of a rule to develop healthy habits: Put dirty clothes in the laundry hamper.

Social Skills

Children develop healthy social skills when there are rules in place to teach them socially acceptable behavior when interacting with others.

An example of a rule to develop healthy social skills: Share your toys with other children.

An example of a rule to develop healthy social skills in older children: The dinner table is a phone/tablet/gadget-free zone.

Real-World Preparation

Family rules can help your child prepare for life in the real world as they grow up. The rules that are set under this category will be different for different children as they depend on the child's temperament. An example of rules to prepare your child for the real world may include rules regarding doing chores, which help develop responsibility, and aid in preparing your child for the working world as an adult.

Family Rules and Consistency

It really cannot be stressed enough just how incredibly important consistency is in your child's life. You need to be consistent across many aspects of their life, such as consistently showing them love. That same consistency is a vital part of upholding family rules when you are dealing with children. Some children may take to rules more easily than others; this comes down to your child's personal temperament. Strong-willed children may need a little more of a helping hand.

- Unstructured routine, permissive parenting, and inconsistently enforcing rules is a recipe for confusion and disaster.
- Being too permissive can offer a child too many choices to make on their own at too young an age. This can leave them feeling confused and overwhelmed which will lead to frequent rule-breaking or acting out.
- Strong-willed children will especially benefit from a slightly stricter approach to enforcing rules. The more consistent you are and the stricter the system, the faster they will learn to adhere to the family rules. Remember to be authoritative and not so strict that you become authoritarian.
- Consistency in enforcing rules creates predictability. When children can predict what is expected of them and also what will happen as a consequence of their actions, they are afforded a sense of security which minimizes outbursts.
- Consistently upholding family rules eventually develops habits, once habits have been developed the rules are followed without your child even having to think about it.

Family Rules and Outside Influence

As a parent, it's your job to raise a well-adjusted and healthy child who will become a functioning part of society when they grow up. This is an especially challenging job when you have a spirited child. It becomes even more testing when you have to compete with the external influences that are playing a part in molding your child's behavior. It has come to light that children actually learn more from their peers than they do from their parents. Surely all of those good values and behavior that you have been instilling in your child from a very young age are there for life, right? Unfortunately, that may not be the case.

- As a parent, you only have a small part to play in your child's overall development.
- Fitting in with peers places children under extreme pressure to behave as their peers expect.
- Children from disciplined and chaotic homes alike are equally susceptible to developing bad behavior if they are exposed to unruly peers from a young age.
- Peer pressure and influence, from pop culture to gangs in the neighborhood, can have more impact on children than even their genetic makeup.
- Family relationships affect the daily happiness of children, but may not do as much to shape your child into who they are going to become in the long run.
- External influences outside of their parental home have a bigger hand in shaping the adults that children will become.
- Children have a need to fit into the culture and external environment in which they are raised, pointing to the reason why children pick up speech patterns and attitudes relating to their peers.

If this sounds like doomsday news for you as a parent, it's not. This information simply highlights the need to expose your child to other children who will be a good influence on them from a very early age. When your child associates with peers who hold the same moral values and exhibit the same good behavior as they do, fitting in with their peers serve to perpetuate that good behavior.

Chapter 9:

Nurturing the Strong-Willed Spirit

Throughout the previous chapters of this book, we have covered everything you need to handle any child irrespective of their temperament; this includes your strong-willed child. We've shown you how to understand your child and how to build their trust, as well as positive ways of parenting and discipline. Now it's time to delve into how to nurture that spirit within your exuberant child while employing all of the effective strategies previously detailed, and some of the obstacles you may face. Remember, you want to raise a spirited child without breaking their spirit.

Strong-willed children are typically confident, smart, and loyal. They show an incredible propensity for thinking creatively and solving problems. They also show a tenacity towards achieving their goals that is admirable, to say the least; however, while these traits may be true of your child, they're probably not what first comes to mind about them. You probably immediately think of their unshakable resolve, iron will, and constantly challenging authority. Some days you may be feeling somewhat hopeless to effect positive change in them; their recklessness can be worrying, and their blatant disregard for your authority can become exhausting.

All of these struggles and emotions can wear you down as a parent and cause you to lose perspective, focusing only on yourself and how you are feeling. However, being able to bring out the best in your child requires a shift of focus solely onto them.

Unseen Needs and Motivators

Strong-willed children are complex and intense; you need to understand the forces at work behind the scenes. Understanding your child helps you to understand what parenting strategies work and which don't.

Your strong-willed child ultimately desires that you respect what they perceive as their right to independence and free will. They perceive everything (like their clothes) as theirs, and feel that they have the sole right to make decisions about those things. Trying to take control away from a strong-willed child leaves them feeling robbed of their right to autonomy, triggering their fighting reaction.

Giving your spirited child even some small measure of control over their life by offering them appropriate choices makes them feel empowered. Learning when to give in and when to hold firm will stand you in good stead when dealing with your child.

Don't Sweat the Small Stuff

Giving in to your child's demands over minor issues isn't the same as giving in to them entirely all the time. It also doesn't equate to losing any of your parental authority. If the issue at hand isn't a big one, it's better to save your battles for the things that do matter. By doing this you are actually building the basis for future cooperation. If your child wants to drag a dirty teddy bear to the store with them, let them. It may not be pretty to look at, but it's not going to hurt them or anyone else either.

When you are faced with larger issues, it is important to win that battle. If it is a matter that will affect their health, safety, or development (such as wearing a seatbelt) you must have the stronger will of the two. If you give in to your strong-willed child on the bigger issues, they will question the effectiveness of your authority and whether it deserves their respect. This is a very slippery slope and sliding down it can happen quickly.

- Children with such a strong will require firm parental leadership that they can respect.
- They are naturally and internally compelled to be defiant in the face of authority.
- Testing authority may be ongoing to prove that it is still there.
- Regularly testing your authority is a means to ensure that it still deserves their respect.

When all is said and done, your strong-willed child must have the understanding that you are the one in charge, you lay down the law, and they must follow it. Powerful children won't learn to control their will and mature emotionally unless they have a strong parent who can stand their ground when necessary despite defiance.

Triggering Defiance

There is nothing that triggers the defiance in a strong-willed child more than having a finger pointed in their face while phrases like, "Because I said so!," "You'll do as I say!," and "You'll do it or else!," ring through their ears. By doing that, you're backing them into a corner and setting a precedent for future defiance, even over little things. If you do not provide a strong-willed child with the respect they desire, you're not going to get any back.

A better solution is to allow them freedom over small things which will count in your favor when it comes to the bigger things. You also need to adjust your thinking. Stop thinking that you are the adult and your child just has to do whatever you say. Children with an iron will are often quite smart. If they don't see a reason for why you are stripping them of their autonomy to make that choice themselves, they aren't going to cooperate. Your approach should be one of firm understanding and persuasion. Remind them that you give them lots of opportunities to make their own choices. Explain the reasoning behind your decision. Tell them that you are not giving in on this decision. Strong-willed children need to feel respected. They are independent, smart, and creative; they understand when you are not showing them respect, and will react accordingly. Barking orders to be obeyed isn't going to get you anywhere.

Another mistake that many parents of strong-willed children make is to react to their child's defiance with anger, and getting themselves all riled up in the process. Losing your cool, raising your voice, and barking orders even more firmly encourages your child to push back against you even more. If they are naturally wired to test authority, it's their natural instinct to defy it even more when they are met with aggression. Your child isn't doing this out of mean-spiritedness; it's just how they are, and watching you get all riled up when they defy you are an irresistible temptation.

When dealing with a strong-willed child, don't trigger their defiance.

- Don't bark orders at them.
- Speak calmly.
- Treat them with courtesy and respect.
- Explain the limitations clearly.
- Don't sweat the small stuff and give them some autonomy.
- Stand calmly firm when addressing important limitations.
- Use questions to encourage compliance.
- Questions imply that your child has a choice, choice means they have freedom.
- Ask questions that require your child to provide a yes or no answer or end the question with "Okay?"

Examples

What not to do, "Clear your stuff off the table!"

Do you see how that comes across as an order being barked by a drill sergeant? There is no faster way to trigger that natural defiance.

What should be said instead is this: "Please clear your stuff off the table," or, "I need to clear the table. Do you want to do that now or in 10 minutes?" or "I need you to clear your stuff off the table, okay?"

See how phrasing an 'order' can come across as a request instead of a command? This shows respect and courtesy to your child. Making a request also naturally requires a calmer tone than giving an order. One of the ways to phrase the request even gives your child a choice which is music to their ears.

Providing a strong-willed child with the chance to obey or not makes a big difference. They may well choose not to obey you, but they are still being given that choice. Their decision to refuse will put you in a position of enforcing consequences, but they will still value the respect shown to them by allowing them to make that decision for themselves.

Respect Their Intelligence

Remember how we keep saying that strong-willed children are smart cookies? Well, they are, and that is another aspect of their personality that needs to be addressed with respect.

They need to know why an activity deserves their effort; convince them of that, and you're already halfway to success.

Motivating a strong-willed child to comply with a request is largely about respecting their intelligence by showing confidence in them, as opposed to insulting it by taking away their freedom of choice.

Even when they make mistakes, these children want the freedom of choice to choose how to fix the situation.

Giving a strong-willed child the opportunity to provide input on the rules and consequences that are made can help to motivate them to obey them.

When tackling a strong-willed child about mistakes, it's best to avoid phrases that will trigger their defiance.

Examples

What not to do: "You forgot to take out the trash again. Go do it now!"

What to do: "You seem to be forgetting to take out the trash. What do you think we can do to help you remember to do it? Let's talk about it after lunch."

Hidden Feelings and Worries

Parents of strong-willed children often overlook that their self-esteem takes a knock, not only yours. Underneath that tough exterior and attitude, there may be a deeper issue at play. It can hurt their feelings to always be saddled with negative labels like being difficult or stubborn. They may be experiencing rejection from peers because they come across as bossy.

- Compliant children typically have higher self-esteem than their strong-willed counterparts.
- Only 17% of compliant teenagers dislike themselves and only 2% had feelings of self-hatred.
- A whopping 35% of strong-willed children dislike themselves and an increase to 8% had feelings of self-hatred.
- Strong-willed children are aware of the difficulties faced by others to get along with them.
- Many of these children secretly fear that their parents, who profess unconditional love for them, will give up on or reject them.
- It is important to reassure a strong-willed child regularly that you will not give up on them and that you love them, especially after wrongdoing.

- Remember that while you are facing difficulties teaching your strong-willed child compliance, they are experiencing difficulties trying to comply. (Wilson, 2014)

Strong-willed children often need more praise for their compliance than naturally compliant children.

Always remember that strong-willed children are not defiant, stubborn, or willful out of a desire to make your life difficult out ill-intent. They are simply wired to be strong-willed by nature. It's not something they chose to be, and they still crave your love, praise, and approval just like any other child. It is important that you don't view your child negatively; doing so will lead you to react negatively to them. They are extremely aware of negativity directed at them and that hurts them just as much as other children, if not more because of their awareness of their naturally strong-willed temperament.

Conclusion

Parenting isn't an easy job by any stretch of the imagination. Your job as the parent of a strong-willed child might be even more challenging than the rest, but it's not impossible! By reading this book, you have received some vital tools to striking that harmonious balance in your relationship with your child. What we've brought to the table is knowledge and, as they say, "Knowledge is power." In the case of raising a spirited child, knowledge is the key to unlocking a good and healthy relationship with your child and making your job as a parent easier and more enjoyable. What's more, the parenting tips and tools provided will help you unlock your child's potential to be the best person that they can be, now and into their adulthood. Building a strong foundation from an early age sets your child up for life-long success in being a well-adjusted, functioning part of the world around them.

What Tools Have We Equipped You With That You Didn't Have Before?

- An understanding of your strong-willed child, their personality, and what makes them tick.
- How positive discipline will set you on the path to success and why it works better than punishment.
- How to implement positive discipline for your spirited child.
- What your limitations are as to how far your parental influence goes while raising your child, and tips on how to overcome obstacles.

- What behavior in your child is age-appropriate, and how to recognize if they are developing normally.
- Reinforcing the fact that you are an authority figure, and how to exert and even regain that authority.
- How to build a trusting relationship with your child.
- How to establish your family's rules.
- Finally, and most importantly, how to nurture the spirit of your strong-willed child.

With all of this information, you are equipped for the task of raising your child more easily and more effectively than before!

Having a strong-willed child doesn't mean you have a bad child. It simply means that you have a unique child, one that needs your understanding, patience, and encouragement to grow and develop. They are depending on you; they need you to know what is contained in this book to help them be the best that they can be. You have a little treasure on your hands, a diamond in the rough. It's now your job to polish that diamond. Remember to look at all the positives of having a strong-willed child and not just to focus on the difficulties that give you a hard time. Your child is still your child, and you are still their loving, caring, and nurturing parent. You need to be their rock and guide them through life. You can do this all-important job of being a parent to a spirited child and now you have the knowledge and tools to help you along the way.

Thank you for taking the time to read this book. If you enjoyed it and learned from it, please leave a review on Amazon so that other parents can be encouraged to read it and learn about their strong-willed child!

References

10 ways we can show respect to our child. (n.d.) The Montessori Notebook. https://www.themontessorinotebook.com/10-ways-we-can-show-respect-to-our-child

15 tips to survive the terrible 3's. (2015, September 8) Childrens MD. https://childrensmd.org/browse-by-age-group/toddler-pre-school/15-tips-survive-terrible-3s

2-3 years: toddler development. (n.d.) Raising Children Network (Australia) Limited. https://raisingchildren.net.au/toddlers/development/development-tracker-1-3-years/2-3-years

7 strategies to build trust with your child. (n.d.). Wahm.com. https://www.wahm.com/articles/7-strategies-to-build-trust-with-your-child.html

Alhassan, M. (2010, September 24). *Why courtesy is important.* Daily Trust. https://dailytrust.com/why-courtesy-is-important

Alli, A. (2018, October 20). *4- to 5-year-olds: Developmental milestones.* Web MD. https://www.webmd.com/parenting/4-to-5-year-old-milestones#1

Benjamin, J. (2015, February). *When your toddler starts testing his limits.* Parents. https://www.parents.com/toddlers-preschoolers/discipline/tips/setting-loving-limits

Blocher, J. (2017, February 21). *Five rules for giving instructions that children will obey.* Center For Anxiety. https://www.centerforanxiety.org/2017/02/21/five-rules-giving-instructions-children-will-obey

Brennan, D. (2019, March 21). *Your child at 2: Milestones.* Web MD. https://www.webmd.com/parenting/guide/child-at-2-milestones#1

Bright Horizons Education team. (2020, January 6). *What is my parenting style? Four types of parenting.* Bright Horizons. https://www.brighthorizons.com/family-resources/parenting-style-four-types-of-parenting

Carrero, K. (n.d.) *Parents who build unshakeable trust with kids have 7 things in common.* Kara Carrero. https://karacarrero.com/building-trust-between-child-parent

Christiano, D. (2019, February25). *What to expect from the terrible twos.* Healthline. https://www.healthline.com/health/parenting/terrible-twos

Common discipline problems and solutions. (2017, July 1). Baby Gooroo. https://babygooroo.com/articles/common-discipline-problems-solutions

Converse, D. (2011, November 2). *Negative discipline is harmful.* Parenting 4 Tomorrow. http://parenting4tomorrow.blogspot.com/2011/11/negative-discipline-is-harmful.html

Cowgill, B. (2029, December). *What's normal for a two-year-old.* Lucie's List. https://www.lucieslist.com/toddlerhood/behavior-normal-two-year-old

Creating rules. (2019, November 5). Centers for Disease Control and Prevention. https://www.verywellfamily.com/types-of-rules-kids-need-1094871

Davis, S. (2017, May 15). *Your Child at 6: Milestones.* WebMD; WebMD. https://www.webmd.com/parenting/guide/child-at-6-milestones#1

DeMattia, J. (2017, August 12). *11 benefits to having a strong-willed child.* Scary Mommy. https://www.scarymommy.com/benefits-to-having-a-strong-willed-child

Dewar, G. (2010-2017). *Authoritarian parenting: What happens to the kids?* Parenting Science. https://www.parentingscience.com/authoritarian-parenting.html

Dewar, G. (2019). *The effects of praise: 7 evidence-based tips for using praise wisely.* Parenting Science. https://www.parentingscience.com/effects-of-praise.html

Discipline and guiding behavior: babies and children. (2019, October 29). Raising Children Network (Australia) Limited. https://raisingchildren.net.au/toddlers/behaviour/discipline/discipline-strategies

Discipline and punishment – what's the difference (4 effective discipline strategies. (2020, June 29). Parenting For Brain. https://www.parentingforbrain.com/discipline-vs-punishment

Editor. (2020, March 26). *When your child talks back: The constructive communication approach.* Industry News Singapore.

https://www.industrynews.sg/when-your-child-talks-back-the-constructive-communication-approach

Encouragement for parent of strong-willed child. (2010). Focus On The Family. https://www.focusonthefamily.com/family-qa/encouragement-for-parent-of-strong-willed-child

Eugster, K. (2007). *Providing structure for your child: How to assert your parental authority.* Kathy Eugster. https://www.kathyeugster.com/articles/article005.htm

Family rituals: what are they? (2017, November 15). Raisingchildren.net.au. https://raisingchildren.net.au/grown-ups/family-life/routines-rituals-relationships/family-rituals#:~:text=Family%20rituals%20make%20family%20members,meaning%20for%20children%20and%20families

Fox, M. (2018, November 5). *Here's what spanking does to kids. None of it is good, doctors say.* NBC News. https://www.nbcnews.com/health/health-news/here-s-what-spanking-does-kids-none-it-good-doctors-n931306

Freeman, D. (n.d.). *5 overlooked strengths of a strong-willed child.* The Joy Filled Mom. https://thejoyfilledmom.com/5-overlooked-strengths-of-a-strong-willed-child

Gillespie, L., & Petersen, S. (n.d.). *Rituals and routines: Supporting Infants and Toddlers and Their Families.* ZERO TO THREE. https://www.zerotothree.org/resources/1808-rituals-and-routines-supporting-infants-and-toddlers-and-their-families

Great Schools Staff. (2009, May 21). *Your child's temperament: 9 basic traits to consider.* Great Schools. https://www.greatschools.org/gk/articles/temperament-traits

Grusec, J., & Danyliuk, T. (2014, December). *Parents' attitudes and beliefs: Their impact on children's development.* Encyclopedia on Early Childhood Development. http://www.child-encyclopedia.com/parenting-skills/according-experts/parents-attitudes-and-beliefs-their-impact-childrens-development

Harold S. Hulbert. (n.d.). Great Thoughts Treasury. http://www.greatthoughtstreasury.com/author/harold-s-hulbert

Intermittent reinforcement. (n.d.). Alley Dog. https://www.alleydog.com/glossary/definition.php?term=Intermittent+Reinforcement

Lansbury, J. (2013, October 23). *The real reasons toddlers push limits.* Janet Lansbury. https://www.janetlansbury.com/2013/10/the-real-reasons-toddlers-push-limits

Lansbury, J. (2014, July 18). *Don't leave testing toddler hanging.* Janet Lansbury. https://www.janetlansbury.com/2014/07/dont-leave-a-testing-toddler-hanging

Lascala, M. (2019, March 8). *What is positive discipline? Experts say this method is effective at getting kids to behave.* Good Housekeeping. https://www.goodhousekeeping.com/life/parenting/a26754534/positive-discipline

Lee, K. (2020, February 13). *Surprising reasons why we need to discipline children.* Very Well Family. https://www.verywellfamily.com/surprising-reasons-why-we-need-to-discipline-children-620115

Lee, K. (2020, May 9). *Consequences for children's bad behavior.* Very Well Family. https://www.verywellfamily.com/list-of-consequences-for-bad-behavior-3867837

Maintaining parental authority. (n.d.) Penfield Building Blocks. https://penfieldbuildingblocks.org/home-and-family/maintaining-parental-authority

Markham, L. (2017, June 8). *How (and when) to apologize to your child.* Psychology Today. https://www.psychologytoday.com/za/blog/peaceful-parents-happy-kids/201706/how-and-when-apologize-your-child

Marks, H. (2010, November 8). 3- to 4-Year-Olds: Developmental Milestones. WebMD; WebMD. https://www.webmd.com/parenting/3-to-4-year-old-milestones

McCready, A. (n.d.). *5 ways to show respect for your child (and gain their respect in return).* Positive Parenting Solutions. https://www.positiveparentingsolutions.com/parenting/5-ways-to-show-respect-for-your-child

McCready, A. (n.d.). *How to teach kids to say sorry: 3 steps for success.* Positive Parenting Solutions. https://www.positiveparentingsolutions.com/parenting/how-to-teach-kids-to-say-sorry

Meduri, A. (2020, February). *Your child's development: 1 year (12 months).* Kids Health. https://kidshealth.org/en/Parents/development-12mos.html

Molineux, J. (2005, March 6). *There are limits to parental influence.* Helena Independent Record. https://helenair.com/lifestyles/there-are-limits-to-parental-influence/article_b8a40421-0acd-5c0c-8add-1bf2bbb8f34f.html

Morin, A. (2019, August 2). *How to use positive discipline techniques. Manage behavior problems in a positive way.* Very Well Family. https://www.verywellfamily.com/positive-discipline-basics-1095043

Morin, A. (2019, July 25). *10 signs you're raising a strong-willed child.* Very Well Family. https://www.verywellfamily.com/signs-raising-a-strong-willed-child-1094963

Morin, A. (2019, September 14). *5 types of household rules kids need.* Very Well Family. https://www.verywellfamily.com/types-of-rules-kids-need-1094871

Morin, A. (2020, March 23). 4 examples of positive discipline. Very Well Family. https://www.verywellfamily.com/examples-of-positive-discipline-1095049

Morin, A. (2020, March 4). *12 ways to become a more authoritative parent.* Very Well Family. https://www.verywellfamily.com/ways-to-become-a-more-authoritative-parent-4136329

Morin, A. (2020, March 8). *Why it is important to discipline your child.* Very Well Family. https://www.verywellfamily.com/why-it-is-important-to-discipline-your-child-1094790

Mulder, P. (2013, October 21). What are 7 C's of Communication? Explanation + tips. Toolshero. https://www.toolshero.com/communication-skills/7cs-of-communication/

Nelson, J. (n.d.). *About positive discipline.* Positive Discipline. https://www.positivediscipline.com/about-positive-discipline

Perry, C. (2019, December 6). *Permissive parenting: The pros and cons, according to a child psychologist.* Parents. https://www.parents.com/parenting/better-parenting/style/permissive-parenting-the-pros-and-cons-according-to-a-child-psychologist

Rongala, A. (2015, July 13). *7 rules of effective communication with examples.* Invensis Global Learning Services. https://www.invensislearning.com/blog/7-rules-of-effective-communication-with-examples

Rules of parenting #21: Forgive and forget: 5 tips on forgiving a child who hurts you. (n.d.). Rules Of Parenting. http://www.rulesofparenting.com/forgive-and-forget-5-tips-on-forgiving-a-child-who-hurts-you

Rymanowics, K. (2017, October, 18). *The nine traits of temperament.* Michigan State University Extension. https://www.canr.msu.edu/news/the_nine_traits_of_temperament

Schreiber, A. (n.d.). *24 reasons children act out – and how to respond.* Motherly. https://www.mother.ly/child/24-reasons-children-act-outand-how-to-respond/theyre-afraid-of-something

Smith, R. (2019, August 26). *How to discipline a strong willed child proven discipline techniques.* Parenting Advisers. https://parentingadvisers.com/how-to-discipline-a-strong-willed-child

Soderlund, A. (n.d.). *How to parent your strong-willed child according to science: Understanding their temperament.* Nurture and Thrive. https://nurtureandthriveblog.com/parenting-strong-willed-child

Stewart, B. (2016, September 27). *What's normal (kinda annoying) 3-year-old behavior and what's not.* She Knows. https://www.sheknows.com/parenting/articles/813862/your-3-year-old-development-behavior-and-parenting-tips-1

Taffel, R. (2012, January/February). *The decline and fall of parental authority and what therapists can do about it.* Psychotherapy Networker. https://www.psychotherapynetworker.org/magazine/article/287/the-decline-and-fall-of-parental-authority

Tamm, L. (n.d.). *Your strong-willed toddler: 3 shifts to turn defiance into cooperation.* The Military Wife And Mom. https://themilitarywifeandmom.com/parenting-strong-willed-toddlers

Ten emotionally intelligent ways to build trust as a parent. (n.d.). Six Seconds. https://www.6seconds.org/2017/08/22/ten-emotionally-intelligent-ways-build-trust-parent

The importance of routine for children. (2017, December 7). KLA Schools. https://www.klaschools.com/importance-of-routine-for-children/#respond

The why's and how's of teaching your child courtesy and respect. (n.d.). Age Of Montessori. http://ageofmontessori.org/whys-hows-teaching-child-courtesy-respect

Tips on helping your child learn to cooperate. (2010, February 20). Zero To Three. https://www.zerotothree.org/resources/222-tips-on-helping-your-child-learn-to-cooperate

Vidakovic, F. (n.d.). *Parenting 101 – practice what you preach (stop being a hypocrite!)*. Inspiring Life. https://www.inspiringlifedreams.com/practice-what-you-preach-parents

Vowles, A. (2012, July 24). *Non-punitive parenting: Could it work for your family?* She Knows. https://www.sheknows.com/parenting/articles/966563/could-non-punitive-parenting-work-for-your-family

Wilson, C. (2014). *What sets them off? Understanding your strong-willed child.* Focus On The Family, Canada. https://www.focusonthefamily.ca/content/what-sets-them-off-understanding-your-strong-willed-child

Wolff, C. (2016, June 3). *Why Having A Strong-Willed Child Is A Good Thing.* Simplemost. https://www.simplemost.com/strong-willed-child-good-thing/

Zorn, A. (November 15). *What to do when being mom makes you feel mean – tips from 10 moms.* Bounceback Parenting. https://bouncebackparenting.com/how-to-let-go-of-anger-10-moms-tips

Made in the USA
Monee, IL
20 January 2021

57583448R00089